Could it be Better?

An unorthodox approach to experiencing more joy and connection in relationships

Cher Anderton, MSW, LICSW

Contributors
Editor: Jon Anderton
Book Cover: Sarah Ward (www.saraward.co)

ACKNOWLEDGEMENTS

El, Will, Jay and Noah: You've been the driving force in my personal healing and growing in order to create safer spaces for you to be you. Witnessing your lives is one of my favorite things and I can't wait to watch more unfold. You're brilliant, beautiful and messy humans and I'm the luckiest to be your mom!

Jon: You've walked with me, in front of me and behind me for over two decades of personal and relationship evolution and have humored countless wild ideas of mine. IFYKYK. Loving you has been one of life's greatest gifts and teachers.

My Village: You're my chosen family and life is beyond rich because of your wisdom, example, embrace, laughter, encouragement and love. Thank you for seeing me, hearing me and loving me. It's a joy to do the same for you!

CONTENTS

 PREFACE

The outline for this book came to me in a dream on January 9, 2022. When I awoke, I quickly wrote everything down in my notes app. I distinctly remember the date, because 2022 was starting off with a bang and I would be leaning heavily, with everything I had, into the tools and strategies you find in this book. The "bang" was being caught off-guard by a proposal of business dissolution by my then business partner and friend. Writing this book became a healthy outlet from what unfolded over an entire year as I worked to protect my life's work up to that point, most of which you will find in this book!

The seed for the book, however, was planted years ago by my dear friend Jessica Peppler, an intuitive counselor and gifted healer. She had a vision of me doing a book signing tour. I dismissed it at the time, because the thought, "Who am I to write a book?" folded into some intense imposter syndrome I was experiencing. All this to say, the book you are reading has been a years-long process and has come from a source bigger than me.

Everything you read in this book is a concept I've learned, a strategy I'm practicing or a skill I'm developing. Everything! I've always loved to learn, even if my high school grades didn't reflect this to be the case (ha!), but becoming a parent took my curiosity and desire to be a better human to a whole new level. For the first decade of parenting, my nervous system was often reactionary. I sometimes felt helpless and incapable, and I was often drowning in guilt and shame for my unskilledness. But every once in a while I would get glimpses of a calm, confident and capable self, and THAT is what I clung to as I made teeny, tiny shifts in what I thought, said and did over time. My "why" for building social and emotional fluency began with my kids and evolved from there. What is your "why?"

Slowly, over years, I learned and unlearned, honing my own social and emotional skills. I will always be unlearning and learning, but the foundation I built from the content you find in this book has been essential in helping me experience more joy and connection as I navigate the trickiest life stuff. I want that for you too! Life is only getting trickier, and in my opinion the way for us to navigate and change is to level up our social and emotional skills. The world needs us to be better, and it's completely within our grasp to achieve. Our kids, our friends and partners, grocery store clerks, the person in front of you on the highway ... they all need us to be better. Everyone deserves people around them trying to move through life in the kindest, most skilled way possible. So let's start learning how to move through life in better ways, together.

INTRODUCTION

Let's Get This Party Started

Listen to Distance *by Emily King*

How is it that we can deeply care for, or even be madly in love with someone, yet experience a high frequency of relational issues with them? How can we love someone, and still have no idea how to skillfully be in a relationship with them? How can we deeply care for and love another human, but not have the skills to show love and make connections in ways they can receive them? Instead, we often hurt those we care about the most. We can feel unskilled in navigating conflict, setting healthy boundaries and/or communicating in kinder ways. We can struggle to practice self-regulation. Lacking relational skills can lead to a sense of dissatisfaction, disappointment and an overall lack of well-being.

Maybe your relationships aren't in dire straits, but they might be lackluster, boring or middle-of-the road. Just ho-hum. And while that might be a comfortable place to exist in at times, it's not necessarily maximizing our time on this planet. Staying comfortable doesn't always support our mental, physical, emotional and relational well-being. Relationships teach us so much about ourselves and each other, about nature, about faith and spirituality and so much more, and if our relationships are just meh, well, then everything else might be too. So your relationships are okay, life is okay, but could they be better?

What might be on the other side of a little (or a lot, you decide) intentional effort? What if intentional effort could invite more ease into our life, because more calm, confidence and capacity often translates into more ease? Humor me for a moment with a video game analogy. When you play video games there are levels, correct? And to master each level, you need to have the knowledge and skills to know where, when and what to do in order to unlock the magic and move to the next level. You see where I'm going with this? There's magic to unlock within ourselves and our relationships, and I'd like to help you do that in some small way. But how?

Let's be clear, most people my age bracket, I'm in my mid-40's, never had a formal education in how to do many non-academic things (like have healthy relationships) in life. WTF. Non-academic skills, sometimes called "soft skills" but going forward we will call them Social and Emotional Intelligence (or Social and Emotional Fluency or Competence), are foundational to our wholeness (the mental, emotional and physical well-being I mentioned earlier) as humans. Because we weren't intentionally and universally taught in classrooms how to do these things, it's no wonder we often struggle as individuals and communities. We have so much knowledge regarding Social and Emotional Intelligence at our fingertips, but it's mostly lost in the ether unless you're an educator, and even then, children are often taught by well-intentioned adults who haven't had their own formal education in these skills. Can you imagine if the educational system operated this way with academics?

Social and Emotional Competencies are skills, knowledge and abilities that help us be successful in ALL of life's arenas. The skills I lay out in this book are what we need to build Social and Emotional fluency, which can lead to some amazing outcomes:

higher levels of academic engagement and functioning; decrease of anxiety and depression symptoms and overall emotional distress; reduction in aggressive behavior, bullying, intimidation and harassment; numerous positive life outcomes; financial benefits across all socioeconomic statuses and demographics; and many more benefits you can find in the Dive Deeper Resources at the end of each chapter.

These evidence-based competencies, well researched by Collaborative for Academic, Social, and Emotional Learning (CASEL) and other organizations, are Self-Awareness, Self-Management, Social Awareness, Responsible Decision-Making and Relationship Skills. Each of these competencies build on the others, meaning I can't develop all the relationship skills I need for well-being if I don't first have self-awareness, self-management (specifically self-regulation), social awareness or know how to make responsible decisions. Now, each of these competencies are books on their own, but I refer to them throughout this book to help you make connections to the strategies I present and the competencies we develop together, particularly the skill of being in relationship with ourselves and others in all of the best possible ways. This is not some liberal bullshit. If you think it is, you can absolutely tell me how the world would be worse off with more humans developing these competencies! As a guide, I've listed each of the competencies, and their general definitions, below.

> **Self-Awareness:** The abilities to understand one's own emotions, thoughts, and values and how they influence behavior across contexts. This includes the capacities to recognize one's strengths and limitations with a well-grounded sense of confidence and purpose.

Self-Management: The abilities to manage one's emotions, thoughts, and behaviors effectively in different situations and to achieve goals and aspirations. This includes the capacities to delay gratification, manage stress, and feel motivation and agency to accomplish personal and collective goals.

Responsible Decision-Making: The abilities to make caring and constructive choices about personal behavior and social interactions across diverse situations. This includes the capacities to consider ethical standards and safety concerns, and to evaluate the benefits and consequences of various actions for personal, social and collective well-being.

Social Awareness: The abilities to understand the perspectives of and empathize with others, including those from diverse backgrounds, cultures, and contexts. This includes the capacities to feel compassion for others, understand broader historical and social norms for behavior in different settings and recognize family, school and community resources and supports.

Relationship Skills: The abilities to establish and maintain healthy and supportive relationships and to effectively navigate settings with diverse individuals and groups. This includes the capacities to communicate clearly, listen actively, cooperate, work collaboratively to problem solve and negotiate conflict constructively, navigate settings with differing social and cultural demands and opportunities, provide leadership and seek or offer help when needed.

Children in the current generation are likely building these competencies through intentional learning and practice at school, yet how many adults are developing them as adults? Most adults have not gotten formal education in these competencies, and this has created a significant skill gap between generations (those of us in our 20's to 50's or later) and a good amount of individual and interpersonal discomfort. It's important to note this should be life work, and not a destination we reach with minimal effort. There should be no getting off this train, and by the end of this book, I don't think you'll want to because of the benefits you'll already be experiencing!

We have our entire lives to learn, unlearn, grow and evolve. Our goal should be to develop relational competence so we can feel more confident navigating life's unpredictable waters, with other humans. What is your vision for what this looks like and sounds like? Do you have models for healthy relationships in your life? There are not enough models in the media (except Ted Lasso), so we need to be really intentional about what information we have coming in. Be choosy about what you consume on social and other media, and about your social circles. Be open to searching for and finding people you admire and aspire to be, and you will find them! Until you have people like this in your life, consider the following actions to help you start.

> **Write down** two or three simple goals or words to describe how you'd like to move through life most of the time, and use these as anchors. For example, I'd like to be more calm, connected and open to possibility in my relationships.

> Get your new goals or words **in front of your brain** as

much as possible. You could, for example, add post-its to your mirror, in your car or on your bedside table.

As you **read your goals or words over and over again,** I invite you to bring up feelings that could be a regular part of your relationships, such as calm, connected and expansive. Sit with those feelings for thirty to sixty seconds. Then go about your day.

Rinse and repeat. You're giving your brain new instructions, allowing it to get on board with any changes in what you think, feel, say and do that you decide to implement after reading this book.

It's our responsibility as individuals and communities, once we know better, to stop trauma and drama through increased self-awareness and self-management, and instead, create more healing and joy-centered relationships by unlearning unhelpful (shitty) wiring (thought, feeling and behavior patterns) and learning new thought, feeling and behavior patterns. We do this by creating habits that promote well-being and through different experiences that reinforce new habits and skills. Sounds like a lot of effort, I know, and it can be at times. AND (a word you will see often in this book because it reminds us many things can be true at the same time) we, and the people in our lives, are worth the effort. It won't always be so hard, and we can make it easier by making teeny, tiny shifts over time. Because, according to the famous Tanzanian Proverb, "Little by little, a little becomes a lot."

What if I told you that by reading this book, by following my writing and conversation prompts and by practicing, practicing and practicing you could feel more calm, connected and joyful in life and in your relationships? You could love and care for yourself better and better? Notice I said more and better in those questions, because here's the thing. In relationships, we are not meant to feel these ways all the time (more on this in Chapter Three) because first, all feelings are okay and meant to be experienced, even uncomfortable ones, and second, we are often in relationship with people who can help us heal our wounds. This can be very uncomfortable at times.

What I am putting forth to you is that if you move through this book as it's outlined, and put some or all of the tools and strategies into practice, you will be more accepting of your humanity and the humanity of others. You will be more whole, compassionate, capable, confident and connected than before. So here's my roadmap for moving through this book.

The book is divided into two sections, with several chapters inside each section. The first section is Self-Discovery (Me), where we develop self-awareness and self-management, in particular. The second section is Relational Discovery (You/We), where we add to your Social and Emotional toolboxes and put everything into practice. The framework of Me/You/We is because I believe it's important for us to understand that any relationship has two (or more) people (ideally healing and skill-building humans) and the relationship itself is the third, or the We, meaning we both/all contribute to the health of the relationship, and without both/all individuals doing so, the relationship suffers. I'm hoping the breakdown of information this way provides a simplified way to understand and move through life and relationships.

At the beginning of each chapter, in lieu of a quote, I give you a mood-setting song to listen to (I already gave you the first song!). I LOVE music. It's a huge part of my well-being and surrounds many of my core childhood memories, so music is fitting to anything I put out into the world. I hope you enjoy the addition of music and that it balances the heavier parts of the book. I even made a book playlist you can access on Spotify via the QR codes at the end of each chapter! I challenge you to make your best guesses as to what lyrics I may be referring to (which I couldn't quote directly for copyright reasons).

At the end of each chapter, you will find additional resources to support the shifts you are making. First, you will find questions for your own self-reflection. These questions can also be used in book club settings to guide conversation. Next, I pull concepts from each chapter to help you as you form new brain wiring and shift narratives. You can create new narratives from the affirmations I offer and/or create your own. Finally, I provide a QR code to guides you to a list of books, videos and more information, where you can dive deeper into the concepts presented in each chapter. I'm hoping this book helps you build a solid foundation upon which you can dig further and further into developing your best self, and better relationships.

In the realm of Social and Emotional Learning (SEL) and psychology, females, members of the LGBTQIA+ and BIPOC communities are under-recognized, and I'd like to help shift that. I believe a massive part of healing and growing as humans must be done through broader representation and interpretation of our experiences. Therefore, I intentionally highlight female and queer experts and authors, as well as people from the global majority in my Dive Deeper Resources. A more inclusive perspective in story and in thought is vital to the expansion of our well-being individually and communally.

One final note regarding the roadmap for the book. You will notice threads of repetition woven throughout the book. This is purposeful. In order to make shifts towards healing and growing as low-burden as possible, we need to get new thoughts and behaviors in front of our brains as often as we can. Also, concepts in this book build upon one another, so references to previously taught tools and strategies makes perfect sense!

Pep Talk to Get Us Started

Our brains sometimes don't appreciate big changes, and this can be a good thing, as massive change is a lot of effort and generally unsustainable for most of us. In this book, I'll identify shifts you can make in what you think, feel, say and do. These shifts require intention (focused attention), and at times might be uncomfortable for you; however, part of what you learn in this book is how to navigate discomfort so it's less intense, versus avoiding the discomfort, which can actually exacerbate it. The shifts you make will help you show up more often for yourself, so you can show up more often for others. Whole, connected relationships are the foundation of our well-being, yet I believe we can't show up relationally in whole, connected ways unless we first show up for ourselves.

What do I mean when I say show up for yourself? I mean we are IN PROCESS, focused on the present and learning to trust ourselves to be okay no matter what happens to us or what mistakes we make. I mean we are emotionally regulated enough that we don't externalize uncomfortable feelings by saying or doing unkind things, or internalize feelings so much we become emotionally unavailable to those we are in relationship with. As individuals, the process of discovering what is helpful and what is not can take trial and error, but that's part of the journey. This book aims to give you the tools to discover what is helpful for YOU so you can master your thoughts and feelings and can say and do better most of the time.

This process isn't about becoming something we aren't, although feelings of inauthenticity may arise when we are doing something new. It's not fake or cheesy, it's just new neural connections in your brain that at first, feel a little weird or awkward. This process is about becoming your best self. It's about uncovering the layers of socialization, experience and story that are not aligned with who you feel you are, feel you could be or feel you want to be. Do you ever wonder who you could be without all of your stuff?

Rewiring your brain is a process where choice is paramount. By the end of this book, I'm hoping you understand the choice you have in creating a life you love, and relationships that add luster to everything you experience no matter what your life experience has been so far. I hope you understand the choice you have in becoming someone you love and are proud of, so you can do what you're meant to do in this life. Take steps to change your wiring so you don't transmit your suffering to those around you.

I want to help and encourage you to walk through the processes in this book, and in the other resources I point you to. AND I want to tell you that as you put in the work, there might be times when you will feel alone because no one will be clapping for you. This might happen because those we are in relationship with might not be accustomed to us showing up for ourselves. When we create healthy boundaries and own our inner power and strength, they might not like what we are doing, or might not applaud us when we want or need them to. Do the work anyway. The work is going to be uncomfortable at first because it's unfamiliar, until it won't be! Discovering the why behind dysfunction in our lives can be painful, but not as painful as the consequences of moving through life unaware, unskilled and wounded. There's a life beyond these things you may not have even imagined. But you're here, so you must have had a little glimpse of what you can experience!

I believe healthy, joyful and sustainable relationships are a creative process between consenting adults. I want you to sit with the phrase creative process and consider what the phrase means to you. To me, it means the sky's the limit. That I can craft whatever kind of relationship I want alongside others, given my values, beliefs, openness to possibility and self-trust. When I'm anchored in self-trust, there is nothing I can't navigate. I stay true to myself, I look after my own safety and needs and I treat myself with love and compassion instead of striving for perfection. There is no magic formula to making relationships work, but there is an art form, techniques that help us master the craft of joyful connections with one another. Techniques that help us feel at ease with ourselves and others. Sounds lovely, right?

Finally, I encourage you to not shy away from change. Healing and growing requires change, and our ability to adapt to our environment is what makes us a highly evolved species. We can be motivated to change through either pain or choice. When we choose to change (heal and grow), we experience less change that is initiated by pain because we have the competence and confidence to navigate tricky stuff that shows up. I believe in your ability to do this, I really do. Thank you for coming to my TED Talk! Let's begin, shall we?

Love Note: This book is for ALL humans. I hope you can see yourself in these words. I love you!

Self-Reflection

- What brought you to this book? Be honest with yourself! Is there room to make your life and relationships better? The answer should always be yes, but what do you want to be better at?
- What are three takeaways you have from the introduction?
- What lyrics from *Distance* by Emily King do you think fit this chapter and why? Message me on social media and I'll select my three favorite responses to win a signed copy of the book!

Affirmations

- I choose to heal and grow to create safer, more joyful spaces for myself and others.
- I can grow my comfort zone by learning to be with discomfort.
- I'm good enough as I am AND I can always be learning how to be a better human. My efforts in this direction are never wasted!

Dive Deeper Resources

Section One

Self-Discovery (Me)

CHAPTER 1

Where We Get Our Stuff

Listen to If I Could Turn Back Time *by Cher*
and I like Me *by Propaganda*

I sometimes (often) fantasize about living by myself on an island. I crave the quiet, the sunshine and waves lapping on the shore with not a person in sight, no one asking me to do or be anything. I crave just me taking care of me. Everyone has this fantasy, right? When I float away into this fantasy, I realize I need to sift through a few things. The need to escape could mean I'm in trauma response (more on this later), it could mean I need more skills to navigate relationships I'm in or maybe it just means I need a fucking break. It's my job to figure this out, because living alone on an island Castaway-style goes against our very nature as humans. Why? Because we are wired for connection.

I'm not saying introverts aren't awesome (I'm one, hi!)! We all have varying needs for connection and that's okay. What you may find in this work of self-discovery, however, is some of your aversion to people, places and connection might be due to early childhood experiences that wired your nervous system a certain way. You will probably come out of this work still an introvert, but you'll hopefully have a deeper understanding of your experiences and the impact they had on the development of your brain and body.

If our ability to connect with others in order to ensure our well-being is so vital, why do we rely almost solely on osmosis to pick up essential relational skills? Especially when most of us picked up relational skills (or a lack thereof) from unskilled people? Lack of intentional social and emotional skill development is evident EVERYWHERE you look, and with everything we know about the brain and body's need for human connection, why aren't we universally and formally teaching fundamental relational (interpersonal) skills in schools and other learning environments alongside academics? As I outlined in the book's introduction, social and emotional skills are in the bedrock of mental and physical well-being.

In order to be relational, many of us need to unlearn disconnecting thought and behavior patterns, and learn new relational patterns. Essentially, we need to rewire our brains in order to experience more joy and connection in our relationships. But before we can consider how we show up in relationships, we need to know more about our wiring, or what we are bringing to the table so to speak. What's our stuff, our shit, our baggage, whatever you want to call it. Let's dig into how we get wired before turning to how to change our wiring. It's simple, but not easy! Those are two very different experiences.

Some of the Ways We Go Wrong

How often do we update the software on our phones? Every few months? What happens when we don't do an update? We get constant notifications, the battery dies sooner than we'd like or there are bugs in how the phone processes. Lack of updating translates into us navigating our phones with a lot more effort than we should be expending. This is a perfect analogy for one of the ways I see us causing harm in relationships. We don't pick up on "notifications" to update our thought and behavior patterns, so our lives and relationships get buggy. Another way of looking at this is if we don't evolve socially and emotionally, we might simply go through life, and specifically relationships, on autopilot. We might phone it in.

Have you ever driven to a place so many times, maybe it's your work commute, to church or to a favorite restaurant, that when you arrive you pause and wonder, "How in the world did I get here?" This is what I mean by autopilot. You have the route so wired into your brain (neurons that often fire together, wire together) you didn't have to think about which turns to make. Your brain just did it for you, which is super cool and efficient for some parts of our lives, but definitely not cool when it comes to relationships, because as you'll learn, some of our wiring (or a lot) is not really relational. We say and do from wounded and/or less-skilled places. We aren't aware that by making teeny, tiny shifts in what we think, say and do, we can experience much better.

Another way we wreak havoc in relationships is when we practice the golden rule. We care for others in ways WE want to be cared for, instead of how the other person experiences/receives care. This is essentially like me speaking Italian to my best friend who speaks Farsi. She might pick up a bit of what I'm putting down, but overall I'll be missing the mark when it comes to connecting. Another way of putting it, we speak our own love languages to others versus speaking their love language to them, and vice versa. It's socially and emotionally immature to think everyone wants to be cared for in the same ways we do. Sure, there are some universal truths about how we should treat each other, but what is your partner's/friend's/family member's definition of kindness? Respect? Affection? What if saying *I love you* everyday to my partner is how I experience care, but my partner responds to acts of service? We might both experience disconnection because we aren't quite hitting the nail on the head. The things I'm talking about are things we try to understand and learn via observation, or past experience, when in reality we are all very unique human beings. Trying to make sense of each other from observation and experience can leave many of us in the dark. The most foundational skill we can develop, then, is to be curious and ask questions of ourselves and each other. Stop trying to be mind readers or mathematicians (past formulas show me if I say or do this, then this will happen) and become more of a researcher who wants to gain more understanding. This then leads to deeper, more connected relationships. I think we can all agree this would be a helpful approach to take in relationships, but what gets in the way of implementation? Not much. Only thought and behavior patterns that were wired into our brains. No big deal.

Each of us has helpful, connecting brain wiring AND each of us also has brain wiring that is non-relational, disconnecting and possibly even traumatizing. What do I mean by brain wiring? When I use the term brain wiring, I'm referring to the neural pathways you have in your brain that are well-worn and efficient, your go-to's or automatic reactions to, and interpretations of, what you experience. I'm referring to the neural connections our brains have developed due to nurture (experience) and nature (genetics) that inform the ways we move through life. Scientists used to believe that once child development was complete, our brains couldn't change. We were who we were. What we now know is our brains have the capacity to be rewired throughout our lives. Yay, we CAN teach old dogs new tricks! Some parts of our brains, such as the hippocampus (memory saver) and olfactory senses (what we smell), even continue to create new cells well into adulthood.

The brain is a stunning display of complexity, and we are learning more and more about it every day. The possibilities are endless. Brain wiring that has us freaking out over any ripple in our proverbial pond? Wiring that says, "You're not good enough, you're unlovable?" Wiring that springs your defense mechanisms into action when your family member says THE ONE THING that triggers the hell out of you? THIS wiring can be changed. The process is called neuroplasticity, a term referring to the brain's ability to change and adapt as a result of experience. Being intentional about what we experience is a major part of rewiring our brains!

Ways Our Brains Get Wired

Check in with yourself now, as some of what you read in this chapter and in Chapter Two could be triggering. I encourage you to ask yourself if you have enough mental and emotional space to dig into where you get your brain wiring from. Before you move on, I suggest you think, say or do something to nurture your nervous systems. If you're not ready, skip ahead to Chapter Three, where I share ways to care for our brains and bodies. If you decide you are ready to proceed, take it slow, take notes and care for yourself throughout. I was careful to summarize at a high level where we get our brain wiring from, with just enough information to increase your self-awareness without getting stuck too much in the weeds. If you want more information, check out the Dive Deeper Resources at the end of this and other chapters.

Genetics

There is a long-standing debate between whether nature, meaning our genetics, or nurture, meaning our environment, is more powerful when it comes to forming human behavior. When it comes to brain wiring, research shows it's not nature OR nurture, it's both. Characteristics (physical traits and behaviors) you are born with AND what you experience throughout your life are both important. Characteristics can impact your experiences and your experiences can impact your characteristics.

Let's talk about genetics. We know we pass down a whole host of things through genetics, including personality traits, driving skills, mental illness and mental health. Research is finding that while there is a relationship between genetics and well-being, the trajectory is not fixed per se. There is a field of study in gene expression called epigenetics which looks at changes in gene expression that don't actually alter your DNA sequence. The ways you carry on a conversation, respond to failure, form relationships with others and generally behave is, in part, related to your genetics (nature), but your world and life experiences also shape your attitudes and behaviors (nurture). The combination of your genetics and experiences ultimately forms your personality and identity, and influences your behavior.

We could go deep down the rabbit hole of genetics, but I'm going to keep it super simple. We come with a set of genes, but we can turn the expression of those genes on and off through our lifestyle choices and experiences. This is a huge equity issue because not every individual has the same opportunity to experience a healthy environment, and we know certain populations experience more trauma and stress. More on this later and in the Dive Deeper Resources at the end of this chapter.

Environment

Where you live and/or grew up has a lot of influence on your wiring. How would you describe the environment you grew up in? Was your community culturally and racially diverse or not? Did you have access to mental health care or did you grow up in an area where getting this kind of help was limited or stigmatized? Did you grow up in a place where healthy food was accessible or not? Could you get medical care when needed? Was education available, high-quality and important in your community? Was your home chaotic and overwhelming, or calm and connected? What were the hidden and not-so-hidden norms of your environment, and which of those norms did you internalize? This is called enculturation, and is essentially a survival mechanism we use to adapt to our circumstances, but as we grow and evolve we may find this type of adaptation to be unhelpful. Enculturation comes from environment, trauma and modeling.

Socialization

Socialization is when we learn to behave in ways acceptable to others. Socialization is more complex in today's world because we have access to more information than we really need, through devices that are so very helpful and also so very unhelpful. As a result, we experience many more NON-EXAMPLES of what is okay or not okay or how to look or how to behave, many of which can be damaging not only for adults but for kids whose brains and bodies are still developing. Look out for some simple tools in later chapters to help you turn down the noise.

Modeling

Modeling can have significant impacts on how our nervous systems react to life. While you may not have personally experienced trauma, your parents or caregivers might have, or they might have just had really cranked up nervous systems due to other factors. This modeling could have become embedded in your own nervous systems. We know children learn by observation, repetition and imitation, so what we MODEL to our kids has way more influence on their development than what they hear from us. Kind of debunks the whole, "Do as I say, not as I do" phrase many of us grew up with. One of the most unhelpful experiences to be modeled to children is emotional neglect. I witness this often in my personal and professional life. If, as children, our caregivers didn't have the skill, will or capacity to tend to our feelings in order for us to co-regulate and learn skills to eventually self-regulate, we internalize this as emotional neglect and carry it into adulthood. We don't care for our feelings as adults.

Take a few moments to write down the five most influential people in your life from birth to age twenty-six. This is the developmental period, broadly speaking, where the brain most easily learns, reorganizes, prunes and solidifies connections. Therefore the people we were around the most at this time in our lives had an incredible impact on our brain wiring. What did they teach you about money? What did they teach you about how to navigate stress, the challenging behavior of others, emotions and relationships with friends, partners, colleagues or bosses? How were you modeled to think and feel about food, movement and health in general? All of this modeling could have been helpful, unhelpful or both. Modeling is especially impactful in the child/parent relationship, because as children, we learn by observation, imitation and repetition. Observation of adult figures and peers, our environment, everything. Imitation of what we observe creates neural pathways that determine how we interpret our lives. Repetition over time strengthens those neural connections.

Please note this is not a blame game. This is simply awareness around where some of your thoughts and stories about yourself, others and life might have come from. It's important to know blame isn't necessary because, as difficult as it may seem, I truly believe most people do the best they can with what they know, AND we know even a parent's best may not be enough for many of us to experience well-being without at least some needed personal healing and growing. Caregivers needn't be villains in our stories. Yes, a lot of the ways we show up in life we come by honestly (because of those caregivers), but if we adopt a victim mentality we can feel powerless to make much needed shifts.

The exercise of identifying what you were modeled and by whom is meant to increase self-awareness you have around where your stuff comes from. Take some time with identification, go with your gut and lay it all out there. Then, as you begin to notice when the identified wiring shows up throughout your day, simply notice it then ask yourself, "Is this old wiring or is this something I choose and want to keep?" See how this simple practice of self-awareness can begin to create new neural pathways and wiring YOU choose.

Love Note: Wondering what you're modeling or have modeled to your own kids? Take a big, deep breath. It's okay. You're okay and you're here! It's never too late to heal and grow, and it's phenomenal modeling to your kids to believe we can always be healing and growing. The latest research shows that if we show up for our kids in the best ways we know how even 60% of the time, they will be okay. When we make repairs for the other 40%, our kids do even better! And, again, we can grow the 60% with intentional shifts in what we think, say and do. I love you. I see you doing the work.

Trauma

A trauma is an event or series of events a person doesn't have the psychological capacity to navigate for a variety of reasons. A trauma can be anything *that is physically or emotionally harmful and has lasting effects on the person's functioning and physical, emotional, social or spiritual well-being.* Complex trauma occurs when a person is exposed to multiple or prolonged forms of trauma. What we know about trauma is it impacts our nervous systems and therefore our relationships, because we are all just a bunch of unique nervous systems interacting with each other! This is why I'm encouraging you to spend time getting to know your nervous system, so you have a better understanding of what you're bringing to the table in relationships.

Whether it happened as a child, adult or both, trauma is relative. Something traumatizing to one person may not traumatize another. All experiences are valid. A really important thing to note about childhood trauma is research used to teach us that what happened to us as kids didn't impact the trajectory of our lives, especially what we experienced as adults. There is now plenty of research saying otherwise. In fact, research now shows what we experience as children directly impacts our adult experience. These experiences can be well-summarized with a particular body of research about Adverse Childhood Experiences (ACEs).

In the mid-1990's, two physicians treating patients with obesity at a clinic in San Diego began collecting anecdotal evidence there was a potential correlation between childhood trauma and negative mental and physical health trajectories in adulthood. The physicians eventually partnered with Kaiser Permanente and the Center for Disease Control to study around

17,000 people, and what they found has informed even more research since the initial study. What research now shows is if you or someone you care for has experienced at least one ACE, you/they are more likely to experience negative mental and/or physical health trajectories in adulthood. Those trajectories look like cardiovascular disease, suicide ideation, substance use, liver disease, risky sexual behavior and poor overall quality of life, and this is by no means an exhaustive list. Research also shows we can experience trauma in ways not yet included as an ACE. It's not about what's wrong WITH US. It's about what has happened TO US.

You can find the ten-question ACEs quiz linked in the Dive Deeper Resources at the end of this chapter. The amount of questions you answer with a yes determines your ACEs score. For example, if you've experienced any type of abuse (mental, emotional, physical, verbal, sexual) or had a parent who suffered from mental illness, used or abused substances, was incarcerated or divorced, then you have ACEs. I don't believe questions about racism and poverty have officially been added yet, but if you've experienced either or both of these, you can add one or two points to your score. If you have a certain amount of ACEs, you are more likely to experience the negative mental, emotional and physical health trajectories I previously mentioned. Research points to a conclusion that the higher the number of ACEs an individual has, the higher the likelihood of experiencing trickier life stuff in adolescence and adulthood. However, something to note is even one ACE can be enough to negatively impact us. The number of ACEs is less important than their actual overall impact. If you are taking the ACEs quiz, please continue to scroll down the website to the Resilience Quiz as well. Resilience factors buffer us from negative ACE impacts, so on one hand, be aware of what might have impacted you from your childhood (ACEs Quiz) but on the other hand, also celebrate and build upon the strengths and protective factors you have (Resilience Quiz).

There are other types of trauma besides ACEs, each incredibly important to note, such as Intergenerational Trauma, Historical Trauma, Racial Trauma, Collective Trauma and more. These types of trauma are common and affect many of you. We need to create safe spaces for healing, and relationships CAN BE one of those safe spaces, as well as dismantle systems inflicting and perpetuating trauma upon so many. You can find out more about types of trauma in the Dive Deeper Resources at the end of this chapter. If you have experienced trauma, please know it is not your fault AND it is possible to heal and grow. I could not do the work I do as a trauma therapist if I didn't see example after example of healing and growing from even the most horrific experiences. Trauma should not define us, but it does shape our narrative AND we have the power to move forward in ways we choose. I hope this book becomes an important part of your journey.

The Impact

What are the results of genetics, trauma, environment, socialization and modeling? Our brains and bodies can often be wired for anxiety, depression, other mental illnesses, interpersonal (aka relational) difficulties, an inability to identify what we are feeling and what to actually do with those feelings. We might experience discontent, physical illness, a fragile sense of self, reactivity to external things and only being okay if things in our lives are okay, and sometimes even when things in our lives are okay we STILL aren't okay. Factors impacting how our brains and bodies are wired influence what we think, say and do all day, everyday. This is why knowing what is going on inside of ourselves (self-awareness) is so important. We can't heal and grow what we don't know is there, so the first step in this process is increasing our self-awareness to identify what we want to be different.

Love Note: You are beautiful, worthy and valuable humans just as you are AND being content with who we are doesn't mean we can't also be consistently evolving. In fact, healing and growing is an act of self-love and resistance to the systems and structures harming us. Healing and growing also makes safer spaces for others to do the same. There is lots of love to go around!

We bring all of this wiring (ME) to relationships, and so does the person who you are in relationship with (YOU). Is it any wonder we have relational issues? Our wiring, especially our trauma wiring, often drives the bus in relationships, meaning our wiring is in charge of how we journey through life versus the parts of ourselves more regulated and focused on connection and logic. Whether we Fight, Flight, Freeze or Fawn (more on these later), dysregulated nervous systems, and the lack of skill to calm them, can negatively impact the way we parent, partner and befriend ourselves and others.

Thank goodness for neuroplasticity! Remember, our brains and bodies are deeply wired for healing and growing, and focusing on our own resilience and ability to change wiring is the foundation upon which we will build. We can create new neural pathways that are our own, and improve our mental and physical health trajectories and our relationships. Wiring we choose, by carefully and intentionally selecting more of what we want to think, feel, say and do. By making shifts to how we think, say and do more often. By making these shifts, we can soothe our nervous systems and train our brains and bodies to not react, but to respond wisely and mindfully. To be more. Think back to the words you chose in the introduction of this book. The words I choose to describe my healing and growing trajectory are calm, confident and capable.

Know Someone Who Has Experienced Trauma?

Because most trauma happens within relationships, it makes sense healing can and should happen in relationships. What often happens, though, is we are in relationships from our wounded parts, and can harm ourselves and others when we operate this way. We can choose a different path. I've already noted trauma to be common, so statistically, each of us are likely to be someone or know someone who has experienced difficult life stuff. And while it's not your job to manage the triggers of people you're in relationship with (it's theirs), you can help create safe spaces for healing. In your interactions, you can help anchor others who have experienced trauma by managing your own stuff and leaning in with gentleness and curiosity. You can provide presence, compassion and steadiness. You can educate yourself on the impact of trauma by reading books, listening to podcasts and asking your partner or friend what it's like for them. People are not their trauma, so learning to hold the right amount of space, while also inviting joy and compassion into the relationship, is deeply fulfilling for everyone, as everyone benefits from more safe, calm, connected and joyful spaces.

Here's the thing, we all have wounds. Every single human has wounded parts of themselves showing up in relationships in wonky ways. Remember the internalized emotional neglect I mentioned earlier? This is an example of a wounding experience but may not be defined as trauma. Just because you haven't experienced an identified trauma doesn't mean you don't have things to heal and grow. Everyone can further develop their social and emotional/relational skill set! Our society, with its violence, division, disconnection, isolation and injustice, is wounding us whether we are conscious of the wounds or not. Something to note is while you may be in relationship with someone who experienced trauma, they are not broken and do not need fixing. Trauma is not an invitation to be a hero and rescue someone. It is an invitation to do your own healing and growing so you can partner with someone in theirs. Journeying together so to speak.

Some of us might be able to experience healing and growing on our own, by listening to podcasts, reading books and slowing down and regulating before we engage in conflict. Many of us, however, need to build our village and partner with professionals in this work. This can look like coaches, mentors, therapists, community groups, affinity groups and so much more. If you have experienced trauma in any of its many forms, I highly suggest finding a therapist. I'm obviously biased here, but partnering with someone whose expertise helps illuminate your path, who understands your very unique nervous systems and helps make sense of what happened to you is invaluable. I've been to therapy myself off and on for years (because therapists need therapists) and it's been one of the most supportive tools I have in my toolbox. There are obviously barriers to seeking counseling, and I want to acknowledge this. Access to resources like therapy is increasing though, AND it still is not enough. I've put resources in the Dive Deeper section at the end of this chapter, some of which might be helpful in your search to find the right kind of support for your healing. Something to note, I believe therapy is for everyone but not every therapist is for everyone. Shop around! Most therapists offer a short, free consultation to see if you are a good fit for each other.

Dear Men

This section could be considered a self-assessment in how skilled you are at managing uncomfortable emotions. If you start to feel some kind of way about what I share here or anywhere else in the book, I absolutely believe in you to have the courage to navigate the feelings, as this is a huge part of our own self-discovery! We can do uncomfortable things!

Males, and even more specifically white males, notice as you move through this section if your brain defends against what I share. This is a section where I invite males to be open to possibility and simply pay attention to what comes up for you. Practice curiosity and ask yourself, "How does this land with me and why?" and "Do the systems Cher mentions harm me (hint: they harm everyone) and how?" Hang in there, because this content impacts all of us (male and otherwise) and our relationships. I'm dedicating an entire section in my book to a specific gender and I have good reason to do so, as you'll see in the coming paragraphs.

Something I believe is very important to hold space for is that until humans accept we all participate in harm in some form or shape, nothing will get better for those who experience the most significant intensity and frequency of harm. I adore all humans, and I simply desire for everyone to experience a fullness of their humanity, as well as the humanity of others. We can't do this unless we excavate and heal the unskilled parts of ourselves to navigate safe, emotionally fluent connection with ALL humans. In the world of psychology, we understand that if what someone else thinks, says or does bumps us (including content in this book!), the discomfort is most often a mirror to the wounded parts of ourselves needing attention. Instead of shying away from the discomfort so we continue to exist in our comfort zones, we can get curious with ourselves and be invited to courageously heal and grow as a human. The costs of existing in our comfort zones, especially in relationships, is too high a price to pay. The value of exploring the waters of social and emotional development, however, is priceless!

Here's why I'm inviting males to pay close attention to their inner worlds and how they impact other humans within the system of patriarchy. Throughout history, men have been socialized to go to great, even violent lengths to establish and sustain "comfort." I put comfort in quotes because it's a false sense of comfort when we have to shut down entire parts of our brains and bodies, often causing harm by doing so, in order to be comfortable. Call it what you will (toxic masculinity for example), but as a result, an entire gender is missing out on deep, trusting, connected relationships with themselves, first, and with others, second. Life and relationships are not a zero sum game. We all lose when we navigate life unskilled and unhealed. When we are willing to build the capacity to expand our comfort zones, instead of staying in the zones society has created for us, everything can expand with it. Our capacity for well-being, through shared power, is infinite, so let's all give a middle finger up to patriarchy and the power over mentality and poisoning of our brains and bodies it perpetuates.

The way our society socializes males (and other genders) to uphold systems of patriarchy often leads men to lack the self-awareness, self-management and social awareness to connect deeply with themselves and others. If you're not familiar with what patriarchy is, "Patriarchy is about the social relations of power between men and women, women and women, and men and men. It is a system for maintaining class, gender, racial, and heterosexual privilege and the status quo of power - relying both on crude forms of oppression, like violence; and subtle ones, like laws; to perpetuate inequality. Patriarchal beliefs of male, heterosexual dominance and the devaluation of girls and women lie at the root of gender-based violence. Patriarchy is a structural force that influences power relations, whether they are abusive or not." (*Asian Pacific Institute on Gender-based Violence, 2023*)

I believe males are missing out on much needed joy and connection because they are more likely to be unable to take relational feedback , have significant defense mechanisms against supposed impermissible emotions, use gaslighting to deflect their own inability to access emotion, self-protect and so much more. What we as a society have done to men through systems of patriarchy and white supremacy has had a significant negative impact on the physical, mental and emotional safety and well-being they experience within themselves and in community with others. The statistics are sobering. Unaliving, or death by suicide, is on the rise among men, especially middle-aged white men. Over ninety-nine percent of mass shootings in America since 1982 have been committed by men, over half by white men, and these numbers are just skimming the surface as to the negative trajectory of the well-being of males in our society.

As systems of oppression, like patriarchy and white supremacy, that have historically (and currently) supported the unskilledness of males are dismantled, men are left bereft. Parts of them might fear not having a place in the world, with the only remedy taking the form of violence against themselves, toward women and people in the global majority, as well as toward queer communities. This violence can appear in small ways, but also in big, horrific ways. Communities at large suffer. There are numerous factors contributing to self-inflicted and community harm, yet I can't help but believe if men chose to level up their social and emotional skill sets, incidents of harm would dramatically decrease. See the Dive Deeper Resources at the end of this chapter for examples of male and non-binary folks who are modeling (not perfectly, but humanly) the development of social and emotional fluency. If you're willing to genuinely lean into this work for your own well-being and the greater good, the door is open for you. If you want to go to therapy, read books and listen to podcasts so you can learn the lingo, then weaponize words to continue to do harm, then please pause here and make a different choice. That's not what this work is for or about!

Love Note: We can experience a lot of growth as individuals AND our healing and growing can be exponential if we ALL lean into it. For things to be different at the community and global levels, we must lean in. Where you are in your social and emotional fluency is most likely not your fault, but it is your responsibility to develop it. Offer yourself and others curiosity and compassion as we navigate this beautiful mess of our lives together. You're a good human AND you can always be better.

Putting It Into Practice

At this point, your brain might be spinning. I believe understanding the whys of healing and growing sets the stage for developing our ability to get to know ourselves in more meaningful ways, so let's dig into some examples and non-examples of social and emotional fluency to get our brains on board with what this can look and sound like in practice.

Non-Example of a Relational Interaction: I had a shit day at work. I didn't take my lunch break because of a deadline, one of my coworkers would not stop dumping their relationship drama on me and I got a call from school saying one of my kids had thrown up. Cool, cool. Some, "Just add it to my list today!" self-talk showed up. I hurried to the school, was not very compassionate to my kiddo when I picked them up and I fumed all the way home. I knew I had a late night ahead of me to meet a work deadline and I wasn't happy about it. When I walked in the door, I started a tirade because everyone's shoes and backpacks were all over the floor, dinner wasn't started even though it was my partner's night to cook and we had a school event later that evening. Tears were shed, disconnection was made and I felt worse after unloading my big, uncomfortable feelings on my family.

Example of a Relational Interaction: I knew I had a long day ahead of me because of a work deadline, so I packed a lunch the night before, something I'd be happy to eat at my desk, I got a good night's sleep and I did a HIIT workout in the morning to wake up my brain and body (self-awareness, self-management). My lunch had some of my favorite things in it to fuel the rest of my crazy day and I listened to some music while I ate. A coworker tried to engage me in some relational drama, but I let them know I didn't have the capacity, smiled, wished them the best and walked back to my office (self-awareness, self-management, social awareness). Even though I worked through lunch, I did take small breaks outside to get fresh air and move my body (Self-Awareness, Self-Management). During those breaks I took deep breaths and noticed little things around me like the breeze and how the leaves twinkled in the sunlight, the sounds of kids playing at the nearby park and how good it felt in my body to take a break (self-awareness, self-management).

When I got a call from school saying one of my kids had thrown up, I was concerned and stressed, but calm as I navigated there and home (self-awareness, self-management). Before I left work, I sent a quick email to my team and boss saying because of an unexpected family situation, I needed until noon the next day to complete the project I was working on. My boss wasn't happy, but I didn't carry her reaction to the situation (self-awareness, self-management).

On my way to the school, I checked my self-talk because some automatic, old wiring was coming up. I used a thought triangle (more on these later) to identify self-talk and feelings, and reworked/practiced them both until my kiddo was in the car (self-awareness, self-management). I rubbed my kiddo's back as I drove home and helped them get set up in bed. My partner hadn't started dinner yet, even though we had an event to go to (he'd had a long day too!), so we quickly made sandwiches, called the rest of the kids to tidy up their shoes and school stuff and headed out to the event. We laughed at what a crazy day it had been, held hands and put on some music, giving us room to take deep breaths and have a break before all of the school event stimulation (self-awareness, self-management, positive relationship building).

I collapsed into bed at the end of the day, but felt proud of how I had cared for myself earlier, allowing me to manage all of the tricky stuff that came up. I got a good night's sleep, headed into work early the next day and finished the project well before lunch. I then took a nice, long lunch at my favorite lunch spot.

Phew! What a difference increasing social and emotional skills can make for ourselves and our relationships! Teeny, tiny shifts in what we think, say and do absolutely pay off over time. Take a moment and write down one of your own non-examples and then rework the scenario how you'd like to show up in the future. No shame. No blame. Just be present and future-focused so you can shift the trajectory of your life and relationships. In future chapters, you'll be provided with tools to manage any discomfort you might have had (I hope you did!) come up during this chapter. I'm right here holding your hand, so gently step forward into the next part of the book.

Self-Reflection

- What are three takeaways you have from this chapter?
- What did you notice pushed at your edges a bit (or a lot)?
- What was your self-talk as you made your way through this chapter?
- What lyrics from *If I Could Turn Back Time* by Cher and *I like Me* by Propaganda do you think fit this chapter and why? Message me on social media and I'll select my three favorite responses to win a signed copy of the book!

Affirmations

- Learning about myself can be uncomfortable, and I am proud of myself for leaning in. I can experience discomfort and be okay.
- I am a beautiful, worthy and valuable human just as I am AND healing and growing is an act of self-love and resistance to systems and experiences harming me and others. I can create safer spaces for myself and others.

Dive Deeper Resources

CHAPTER 2

How Our Wiring Informs
How We Move Through Life

Listen to Never Too Much *by Luther Vandross*

Now that you have a deeper understanding of where your brain and body wiring comes from, we want to pay attention to how wiring informs our attachment style and our core beliefs. Both of these highly impact our ability to connect with ourselves and others!

Attachment Basics, the Outcomes of Our Experiences

You may have heard the term "attachment style" at some point in your life. Attachment style refers to the thought and behavior patterns we have in relationships. Why does our attachment style matter? Because it shows up, and will show up, in EVERY relationship you're in or will be in, and your attachment style was determined by *if* and *how* your needs were met as children. Again, no blame game (our parents aren't the villains here!) but simply information to increase your self-awareness. I'm going to greatly simplify attachment here, mostly because there is already a lot of information out there. We also don't need to know a lot in order to identify which attachment type(s) we are, what our attachment style looks and sounds like in action or what skills we need to shift from an insecurely attached state to a securely attached state (the goal!) more often. Let's begin with identification. You may already be aware of your attachment style, or you may have no idea what I'm talking about. Either way, get a fresh perspective by taking the quiz in the Dive Deeper Resources at the end of this chapter. Someone with a Secure Attachment style will more often than not exhibit the following:

- Positive sense of self
- Healthy amount of reliance on themselves to feel valued or loved
- Feels good on their own AND enjoys connection and intimacy with others in healthy ways
- Ability to create trusting, long-term relationships

We want to slowly but surely shift away from the following attachment styles:

- Avoidant: Tend to avoid intimacy, have dismissive attitudes towards social and emotional interactions/topics and struggle to ask for help.
- Anxious/Ambivalent: Can be perceived and experienced by others as needy or clingy and may require constant validation and reassurance in the relationship.
- Disorganized (Anxious/Avoidant): Most likely experienced childhood trauma or some other type of inconsistency growing up, such as moving constantly. Indicates a person has little to no real coping strategies and experiences a significantly reduced ability to navigate the world. Desires to be loved and are fearful of vulnerability and connection which are necessary for experiencing love.

An important thing to note is most of us do not operate from a place of insecure attachment all the time. We get TRIGGERED into insecurely attached states by others saying or doing something to us, or some other experience. One minute, we're cruising along feeling pretty good in a relationship, until our friend doesn't text us back in a timely manner, our partner goes out with friends to a bar or we get a dismissive look from our boss and boom! Certain behaviors, feelings and thoughts activate our nervous systems, and our brains and bodies move into an insecure place. Here's the tricky thing, we might be in an insecure place because we fear we aren't lovable, or we will be rejected or abandoned, and then we think, say and do from an insecure place. We might text incessantly, interrogate our partners to see if they were faithful, check out from social engagements or behave in other ways that communicate we are in an insecure place. As a result, and unfortunately, we often end up creating the very thing we deeply fear because those behaviors are difficult to experience over and over in a relationship and don't feel good to either party involved. Relationship can end up in a strained place or cease to exist altogether. So, how do we shift our attachment style to be more secure, more often? Here are four steps that should help.

Disrupt the Pattern: What is one of your greatest relationship fears? That you'll be rejected? Abandoned? That you're unlovable? Make a note of behaviors you have that might result in these fears actually happening and zoom out a bit. Observe the behaviors like a scientist and get curious.

Use A Thought Triangle (more on this later): What are one or two behaviors you identified you'd like to change? What can you think, say or do to shift behavior to teach your nervous systems new ways of being in relationship? (HINT: the steps for healthy emotion processing from Chapter Four come in handy here)

Practice, Practice, Practice: All of this work takes self-awareness and intention. Little by little, a little becomes a lot! Also, most of us have lots of opportunities to practice in our relationships!

Invite People in Your Circle to Hold Space for You as You Heal and Grow: Say something like, "Hey (insert name), I notice I get triggered into an unhelpful space sometimes and I (insert behavior/s). I want to make you aware that I'm aware, and if you can, please be patient and compassionate with me as I figure this out."

It's not anyone else's job to not trigger you AND people who care about you and have the skill, will and capacity to do so, can also pay attention to their own behaviors and try to make shifts that are in alignment for them. You can make the request, but not the demand!

Core Beliefs

Beliefs about ourselves and others are another outcome of the wiring we get from the modeling, genetics, socialization, environment and trauma we have experienced. Remember, even in adulthood, much of our wiring, and as a result many of our beliefs, is not our own unless we've done a significant amount of work to heal and grow already. Beliefs are one of the ways our brains make sense of and navigate our complex human experience. They are mental representations of the ways our brains expect things in our environment to behave, and how things should be related to each other, or in other words they are the patterns our brain expects the world to <u>conform</u> to. Beliefs are templates for efficient learning and are often essential for survival. Beliefs are programmed into our psyche, much like a computer has programming. A computer doesn't question programming, it just is, and this is how beliefs influence how we move through life, on the autopilot I mentioned in the last chapter. Our autopilot, or unconscious wiring, occurs because certain neural connections have fired together so many times, they have wired together to become memorized, almost robotic ways of moving through life. Thankfully, with more self-awareness we can question and change our programming without any outside influence, without someone else typing in the code. Once we uncover what our core beliefs are, we can change them by choosing new ones, with new words and new language. We might have less helpful beliefs to us and others. We might have beliefs harming our mental and physical health, such as "I'm lazy," "I'm not good enough," "I can't get what I want," or "I can't handle this." We might have beliefs disconnecting us from others, especially those who look, sound, behave or believe differently from us.

We need to regularly examine beliefs to make sure they are chosen, supportive of our well-being and supportive of the well-being of the community at large. If you find you have beliefs you'd like to shift, you can simply choose new ones and find evidence for those beliefs to be true for you. This practice takes time, and can greatly benefit you and those you are in relationship with. We can consider the ethical implications of our beliefs. Are our beliefs inclusive and loving? Do our beliefs allow humans the dignity of making choices for themselves? We often experience our beliefs as truth, because we've thought them so much they FEEL factual. But there is a distinct difference between facts and beliefs. Facts have evidence and can be proven. Beliefs can be formed DESPITE evidence to the contrary, meaning if your beliefs don't serve you and the highest good of other human beings, then you can replace them with beliefs that do.

Core beliefs are our innermost deepest, darkest secrets. We don't typically walk around saying to ourselves and others, "I'm not good enough" or "I'm unlovable," but our behaviors tend to communicate these beliefs anyway. We each have all kinds of thoughts entering our mind space, then leaving our mind space. We also have all kinds of thoughts entering our mind space and never leaving, in fact they get thought and thought over and over again, and over time, these patterns of thinking solidify into beliefs. Those beliefs then become the lens through which we see and interpret every experience and every interaction. So if I have picked up the belief I'm unlovable somewhere along my journey, then the parts of me that feels unlovable shows up in all kinds of ways. I might self-sabotage relationships, not practice self-compassion and much more, essentially subconsciously looking for evidence to support the unhelpful beliefs.

For example, if we didn't have parents or caregivers who could coach us through big, uncomfortable emotions, and we were instead told to stop being dramatic and "get over it" (this is an example of gaslighting), we might internalize these experiences as a wound and potentially a belief we are "too much" for others. As a teen or adult, we might not communicate our feelings and needs in relationships because we don't want to be perceived as too much. We might minimize our experiences and feelings, or we might attract someone who reinforces narratives that we are too much. We might also opt out of relationships before the other person leaves us, because our story is they most certainly will leave us when they find out how we are too much.

To heal in this particular example, first, we need to uncover the story. You might go to therapy to do this, or you might do enough self-reflection and self-discovery to see the story yourself. Once you recognize you have a story telling you you're too much, you can decide if you want to keep the narrative. Is it helpful? Does it support you having healthy relationships? Do you feel grounded and in your body, connected to yourself? Not at all. In fact, when you sit with yourself and hear the self-talk, "I'm too much, I can be safe by being quiet," you may feel anxious and buzzy in your chest, your head spins a bit and you feel nauseated. Definitely unhelpful, because who wants to feel these ways in their body. Some professionals will encourage you to ask yourself if a belief is true for you. Of course it feels true because it's wired into our brains! I suggest you avoid this question and instead ask yourself more helpful questions such as, "What belief do I WANT to be true for me?" and then do the work to install your chosen beliefs to replace old, unhelpful ones.

The next step would be for you to determine new narratives you prefer to have wired in your brain instead. You might choose something like, "All feelings are okay and I'm learning healthy ways to express them. I can ask for what I need and want." Then sit with your self-talk for a moment and tune into your body. You might still feel anxious and buzzy, but less intensely. You might feel hopeful, self-compassionate and focused. This self-talk might feel true to you at a five (on a scale of 1-10, 10 being 100% true). You could write down your new self-talk on post-it notes and put them around your house and car to get them in front of your brain as much as possible.

Another layer of healing can come from increasing your self-awareness when the old story shows up. Pivot, then practice your replacement self-talk. "All feelings are okay and I'm learning healthy ways to express them. I can ask for what I need and want," then say and do from this new story versus the old one.

We Can't Change What We Don't Know Is There

One of the most incredible modalities I use as a therapist, besides Internal Family Systems, or IFS, is Eye Movement Desensitization and Reprocessing (EMDR). In the preparatory stage of EMDR, we (therapist and client) go through a list of negative cognitions to bring them from the subconscious mind to consciousness. A major aspect of therapy, and EMDR specifically, is to replace old, harmful beliefs/thoughts about ourselves and our world. Most of us aren't aware of the unhelpful core beliefs we operate from, so knowing what they are and then feeling empowered to change them (our superpower) is a step in the right direction. I ask my clients, while I read the following list, to react to me from their bodies, and not from the overthinking parts in their head. Your body will tell you if it's a yes or no when hearing the following list of negative core beliefs:

I am something wrong
I don't deserve love
I am a bad person
I am terrible
I am worthless (inadequate)
I am shameful
I am not lovable
I am not good enough
I deserve only bad things
I am permanently damaged
I am ugly (my body is hateful)
I do not deserve
I am stupid (not smart enough)
I am insignificant (unimportant)
I am a disappointment
I deserve to be miserable
I am different (don't belong)
I did something wrong
I should have done something
I did something wrong

I should have known better

I cannot be trusted

I cannot trust myself

I cannot trust my judgment

I cannot trust anyone

I cannot protect myself

I am in danger

It's not okay to feel (show) my emotions

I cannot stand up for myself

I cannot let it out

I am not in control

I am powerless (helpless)

I am weak

I cannot get what I want

I am a failure (will fail)

I cannot succeed

I have to be perfect (please everyone)

I cannot stand it

I am inadequate

I cannot trust anyone

There's something wrong with me

Any of these statements surprise you? Did your body react to any? Maybe you didn't know what was floating around in your psyche. These discoveries can be uncomfortable AND now you know they are there, you can do something about them! Beliefs such as these have most likely been guiding how you show up in life, so now you can REALLY shift the trajectory of your well-being. Here's your chance to discard other people's fears and limitations, as well as your own fears and limitations. Replacing unhelpful beliefs is as SIMPLE as replacing them with new, chosen, positive ones. However, it's not as easy as just this. First, we need to be aware of when old beliefs come up in order to replace them. Then we can be both proactive and reactive to change those core beliefs. Remember, the way our brains and bodies are wired, including our attachment styles, informs what we believe about ourselves and the world. Our beliefs guide so much of what we think, feel, say and do. All beliefs are okay EXCEPT beliefs harming ourselves and/or others. We can have all kinds of wonky wiring making what we believe move us towards division within our brains and bodies, as well as in the community around us. I've gone through and continue to go through the practice of uncovering beliefs harming myself and others. It's very uncomfortable work! I've felt embarrassment, humiliation, shame, guilt, disappointment, disgust and horror as I've uncovered certain beliefs, and guess what? I'm still standing. In fact, I'm thriving because I'm practicing the tools and strategies necessary to navigate the process. I love myself and others even more than before because I've learned to be with uncomfortable feelings, take the information I need from them, then do the needed healing and growing.

Love Note: Here you are, showing up for you and doing the most to, little by little, bring what has been lurking in the background of your psyche to your awareness. This is no small thing AND it can be so uncomfortable! I'm proud of you. I really am! Now that you know what is there you can love yourself forward by offering compassion to the parts of you picking up these beliefs along the way. You can choose a new way forward and decide to be good enough just as you are. You can decide you are lovable, worthy and significant. I truly believe you are! Feel free to ride my coattails for a while if you need a lift towards believing it for yourself. Soon enough you can be the coattails for someone else!

Putting It Into Practice

We see some friends posting about a lunch we weren't invited to on social media and start having FEELINGS. You know the kind ... rejection, hurt, feeling left out and sadness. These feelings are really uncomfortable in the brain and body. These feelings reinforce wounds we have around being rejected and abandoned, so the discomfort intensifies. When we notice this happening, we pause and check our self-talk. We replace unhelpful narratives like we are too much or we are unlikable with, "This is feeding the old belief I'm unlikeable/unloveable and I don't choose the belief anymore. My chosen belief is I am likable and loveable and I have evidence for this because ..." Then we would go on to find evidence in our lives of our likability and loveability. We change the old, subconscious belief by consciously changing the language we use. When we change unhelpful beliefs, we shift our mindset and move through life in more loving and compassionate ways. While self-compassion isn't often the first response to uncomfortable experiences, the work you're doing now can disrupt those patterns and guide yourself towards new, more self-compassionate ones!

Self-Reflection

- What did you identify as your attachment style when triggered?
- What are some of the triggers you're already aware of moving you into an insecure place?
- What are some factors helping you stay in a secure place as often as possible?
- What core beliefs do you want to shift first? Start with one or two at the most because you don't want to overwhelm your brain!
- What song lyrics from *Never Too Much* by Luther Vandross do you think fit this chapter and why?

Affirmations

- As an adult, I have the responsibility to uncover unhelpful beliefs and choose new ones aligning with my values. What a gift!
- I choose a new way forward and decide to be good enough just as I am. I choose to believe I'm lovable, worthy and significant.

Dive Deeper Resources

# CHAPTER 3

Bringing Attention to
What We Think, Feel, Say and Do

Listen to My Future by Billie Eilish

In the last chapter, I hope you developed greater self-awareness around attachment styles as well as uncovered unhelpful core beliefs you have lurking around in the recesses of your brain. In this chapter, we are going to dive into a new tool to help you shift pesky core beliefs no longer serving you AND help you move towards more secure attachment experiences more often. The tool I'm talking about comes from a therapeutic modality called Cognitive Behavioral Therapy (CBT), which was developed by Aaron Beck. The model focuses on changing thoughts (cognitions) and behavior (what we say and do) in order to change how we feel.

A tool I believe everyone should have in their Social and Emotional Toolbox is a Cognitive Behavioral Therapy thought triangle. A thought triangle is a visual representation of how our thoughts affect our behavior and feelings, and how our behavior affects what we think and feel. If we change any point of the triangle, meaning if we change what we think, feel, say and/or do, the other points of the triangle change too. Our internal thought triangles can be helpful (kind, supportive self-talk, comfortable feelings) or unhelpful (critical, mean self-talk, uncomfortable feelings). When we notice a triangle needs to shift, meaning we want to change what we think, feel, say and/or do, a solid place to begin is by shifting a thought or behavior first. Both of those points of the triangle shift the way we feel most effectively. Below you'll find a visual representation of the CBT thought triangle.

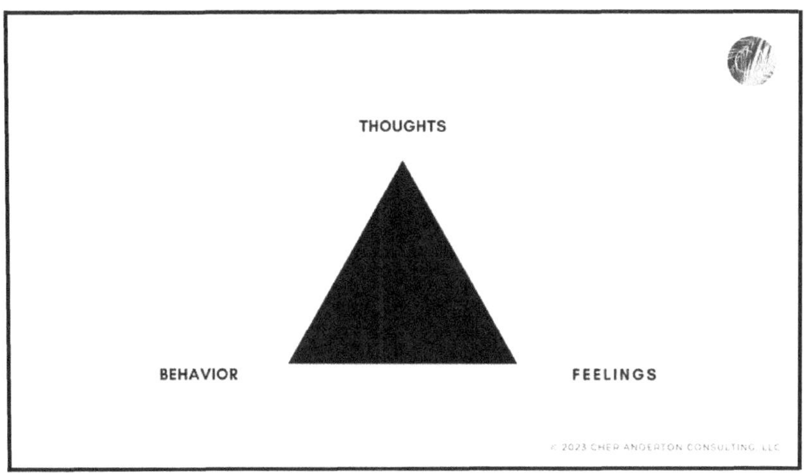

Let's start with several examples of unhelpful thought triangles, which I'll rework in the next chapter to give you a sense of how they can be shifted.

Initial Thought: I need connection but my partner is ignoring me. I keep trying to get their attention and they're not noticing. They don't care about me.
Feelings: Defeat, frustration, anger, betrayal, shame, rejection, sadness
Behavior: I withdraw, I make passive aggressive comments, I ignore him too or, because I have an ambivalent attachment style and I might be triggered, I pester him for attention and connection.

Initial Thought: My workplace is toxic but I can't look for anything else because I don't have the experience other people do.

Feelings: Defeat, despair, hopelessness, powerlessness, resignation, feeling trapped

Behavior: I stay in a job that harms my mental and physical health, I complain all the time to anyone who will listen, I have a hard time being productive at work, I'm so exhausted after work I hardly have a social life.

Initial Thought: I can't make healthier choices. Every time I try, I fail.

Feelings: Powerlessness, stuck, sad, angry, stupid, embarrassed

Behavior: I give up, don't bother trying, I judge or envy other people.

Thought Triangles: Thoughts Breakdown

Not the most helpful thoughts! Luckily, every human being's superpower is to shift our thoughts to be more helpful. When our thoughts are more often helpful than not, our brains and bodies feel better. When we feel better, we say and do better. When we say and do better, we think better, and so on. It's a cycle that fosters wellness. Shifting self-talk, in other words our thoughts, is key to unlocking more joy! We have so much choice regarding the thoughts we allow to stay in our brain space, and with a few tweaks to our self-talk, we can significantly shift what we experience in our brains and bodies.

We all have a mix of both helpful and unhelpful thoughts, and one of the most important things to note is WE ARE NOT OUR THOUGHTS. Our thoughts are not true in the way we believe them to be at least. We actually have a choice whether or not to allow thought popping into our heads to stay in our brain space. We entertain thoughts, we think them over and over again and before we know it, we've made them "true" for our brains. A thought is just a thought. But a thought being thought over and over again becomes a pattern, and patterns become beliefs. And we can end up believing some pretty wild shit about ourselves and others. Remember, much of what we think or say to ourselves (self-talk) comes from our childhood experiences (see previous chapter on where we get our wiring), so our brains are often living in the past or trying to predict the future (hello anxiety), basing our interpretations of the present moment on very young, often childlike stories. This can be really problematic in relationships! If what we are saying and doing in relationships comes from thoughts and feelings created and reinforced in childhood, no wonder we struggle!

Thought Triangles: Feelings Breakdown

A common practice as a therapist is to invite clients to pause and tune into their bodies so they can notice what is coming up for them at the moment. Clients often want to scoot past feelings and keep talking as a form of self-protection. Some of our parts believe that if we stay in our heads (where the talking happens) then we can avoid emotional distress. Not so my friends! Emotions not being connected with and attended to become trapped and come out sideways, and most often, if not always, in very, very uncomfortable ways. If we want to experience the fullness of our humanity, and the humanity of others, we must practice accepting the full range of our feelings and helping them move through, and out of, our bodies. Breathe. Then let them in and let them out.

We feel feelings in our bodies, not our brains. Our brains are where the thoughts are, but often we confuse the two. For example, when I ask clients to identify what they are feeling they often reply with a thought instead. I get it. Noticing what is happening in our bodies can be tricky and even downright intolerable. It's okay! Start where you are with this practice.

You'll notice I use terms like comfortable and uncomfortable to describe feelings. Often feelings are referred to as good or bad, positive or negative, but I don't believe feelings exist in those categories. We are taught to believe this, but a reframe/rewiring is helpful here. Let me unpack what I mean by comfortable and uncomfortable. Because we feel feelings in our bodies, we can either be having a comfortable experience or an uncomfortable one, our bodies rarely feel neutral. While a lot of people might say discomfort is a bad thing, I don't believe it to be so. Saying discomfort is a bad thing is a childlike story. As a child, uncomfortable feelings felt really bad because we didn't have the skills we have as adults to let the feelings in and then out. Our adult story can be, "I can manage discomfort and build the skills I need to tend to my feelings." Discomfort can move us in really wonderful directions, including towards overall wellness. How intensely we feel feelings, and how often we are uncomfortable, are possible indicators we need to level up our emotion regulation skills.

I get comfortable feelings are what we want to have most of the time, but all feelings are okay. Feelings are just information! What matters most is what we say and do with our feelings. For example, we don't want to be mean with our mad, or hurt people with our sad. Feeling uncomfortable feelings is not an excuse to say and do whatever we want to whomever we want. Just because I'm mad or frustrated doesn't mean it's okay to cut someone off in traffic, yell at my kids, slam doors, stonewall my partner or pop off in the comments section of someone's social media post. Just because I'm hurt doesn't mean I call the person who hurt me an unkind name, poke at their vulnerabilities, post about it online, call the person out or ghost them.

On a very simple level, feelings are signals from our brains telling us things are either okay or not okay. Feelings are a way to get our attention, again sometimes in very uncomfortable ways, but this doesn't make them bad. Those feelings just ARE. It's the meaning we give our feelings and the experiences connected to them bringing on the suffering. All feelings have a purpose. Feelings can motivate us, help us make choices, help us connect with others or ourselves and signal alignment with our values or not. We need feelings, including the uncomfortable ones, to guide us but instead we do a lot to avoid, ignore, distract and numb ourselves from uncomfortable, and even sometimes comfortable, feelings. We normalize too many behaviors moving us away from well-being. This is often because most of us haven't received a helpful education on how to navigate uncomfortable feelings, so we cope with them in ways we were modeled and taught as children, or in ways we picked up along the way.

Ignoring, stuffing down, avoiding and distracting can look like parts of ourselves taking us out of our bodies through dissociation, engaging with harmful substances (also forms of dissociation), self-harm, shopping, eating, busy-ing and perfectionism, among others, so we don't have to experience the discomfort of say, anxiety. Honestly, most of us will do ANYTHING to not feel uncomfortable feelings and it wreaks havoc on ourselves, our relationships and on society globally. And here's the kicker, we need the information our feelings provide in order to live our best lives and be in better relationship with others. Our bodies are so very wise! These vessels we exist in have so much information to impart to us and because of our unskilledness, we miss out on so much wisdom! No more! Let's change these narratives, because the benefits of practicing self-attunement and having healthy coping strategies to manage whatever comes up are endless!

Love Note: Many of us developed coping strategies as kids in order to survive harmful things happening to us. What clever children we were! It's really important to honor the ingenuity of our younger selves. At the same time, we can let those little ones know we don't need those strategies anymore. We can let them know we want to practice new ones.

When it comes to feeling our feelings and developing helpful coping strategies, we may need to move slowly. Parts of us can get really triggered if we don't move gently towards connecting with our bodies' feelings. Tuning into our body's internal world (thoughts, feelings) is often not a comfortable experience. If this is the case for you, then I suggest you meet yourself where you are. Over time, feelings can become less intense because we notice them earlier. Feelings can be just like a newborn baby trying to get its caregiver's attention. At first, a baby's fussing might be subtle, but if it goes unaddressed, well, we all know what a baby who is losing their shit sounds like! If we don't notice signaled feelings early on, they often intensify until we can get really uncomfortable (like the baby who screams to get its needs noticed and met). This is no fun for anyone! So the more skilled we become at noticing feelings, especially uncomfortable ones, the less discomfort we experience down the road. Let's begin sensing, identifying and practicing the following steps (1-4) to help build self-awareness of your feelings. If you're up for additional work developing self-awareness around your feelings, try steps 5-7.

- **Print out the Gottman Feelings Wheel** (linked in the Dive Deeper Resources) or another feelings chart you connect with. There are lots of free ones on the internet. Make several copies and place them around your home, car and work space. Remember, when we are disrupting patterns of unawareness, we need to remind our brains of our new path towards awareness with visuals, whether this is pictures or calendar alerts or whatever works for you.

- Once the chart is in front of you, **identify the three to five feelings** you feel most often. Then consider, what you prefer to feel other to feel other feelings more often? When I ask clients this question, often in our first session, almost one hundred percent of the time the feelings they want to get more of fall under the categories of calm, confident and capable. This is why you hear me mention those felt experiences so often throughout this book! But what would YOU choose? Now, we can't feel these things all of the time, but we can feel them more of the time! Repeat after me, all feelings are okay. What we say and do with our feelings matters most.

- Next, **ask yourself in what contexts do you experience the feelings you want more of?** At work? With a certain friend or family member? What activities or interactions do you engage in that elicit these feelings most often? Make sure you note the activities and interactions you identify so you can add them to your Feel Good Plan, a concept I will introduce to you soon.

- We also want to **bring awareness to activities and interactions** eliciting uncomfortable feelings we wantless of. Take some time to identify the activities and interactions you want less of. You will learn how to have less of them throughout this book! Stay tuned.

- **Create a practice** of tuning into your feelings throughout the day and/or week. If your body is uncomfortable with you noticing what you're feeling, start with once a day or a few times per week. Keep the practice simple and as low burden as possible. Many of my clients stick with their feelings chart to guide this practice, while others, especially my teen clients, enjoy using apps to support this practice. If you search feelings in the app store, you can search through dozens of apps to find one fitting your needs and wants. There are even CBT related ones!

- Part of **our ongoing practice is paying attention** to what we are feeling, how intensely we are feeling and where in our bodies we are feeling the feels. We can do this by asking ourselves the following questions:

What am I feeling?
On a scale of 1-10, what number would I give the intensity of the feeling?
Where do I feel these feelings in my body?

- **We can feel all kinds of feelings,** uncomfortable and comfortable, at the same time! Our brains and bodies are so complex, but we want to welcome and get used to holding space for all of our feelings.

There are feelings we experience that can be almost unbearable, like shame and shame's buddy, guilt. Shame tells us, "I am something wrong," while guilt tells us, "I did something wrong." Experiencing shame throughout life is inevitable AND it can guide us towards what needs to be healed. Guilt is actually a really helpful feeling helping us shift behaviors. When you experience guilt, use it as a prompt to evaluate what you're thinking, saying and doing. Consider this a self-inventory without getting too stuck in the discomfort. A self-inventory can include asking yourself the following questions:

What happened that triggered the shame or guilt? Just state facts here.

What story am I telling myself about what happened? What am I thinking, saying or doing that needs to shift?

Do I need to make a repair, and if yes, how? How can I show myself and the other person compassion in this moment? (See later chapters for how to make a repair!)

Once you complete your evaluation and inventory, you may want to shift something, or you may find your guilt is associated with an old story and you can let it go. Hopefully these reframes and definitions invite you to be more curious next time those difficult feelings show up.

Thought Triangles: Behavior Breakdown

Behavior is simply what we say and do. We all have behaviors we are conscious of, especially when we are learning new skills, and behaviors we are unconscious of, meaning they happen automatically. For example, when we learn to drive we have to be conscious of what we say and do to get from one place to another. Once we have more skill, we often get from here to there without even paying attention. We end up at our destination without our brains really being present. We could have been thinking of the fun weekend we had, or the hard conversation we need to have with a colleague, instead of paying attention to the turns, the speed or the traffic. Simplistically, a way to change behaviors not conducive to our well-being and our relationships is to bring attention to our thoughts and feelings. Then we can make little shifts to guide us towards more relational behaviors.

From my perspective, there is no such thing as good or bad behavior, only connecting or disconnecting. I also use terms like relational or non-relational. Skilled or unskilled. Moving away from the good/bad binary serves a few purposes. First, those of us raised in black and white environments can move away from shame coming from the use of words like bad to describe behavior. Second, we can make healthier connections and behavior changes if we focus on what's truly worth paying attention to, and how our behavior impacts us as individuals and those we interact with. Categories I use to describe behavior are all on a spectrum, and where our behavior lands on that spectrum depends on a lot of things, like our belief systems and other wiring. I've detailed a few things to note about behavior below.

- Misguided (aka disconnecting) behaviors communicate an unmet need and/or a lagging skill.
- All behavior serves a function (meets a need). The four functions of behavior are attention, escape, tangibles (access to an item or preferred activity) and/or sensory (input and output).
- We need an understanding of the nature and purpose of behavior, an understanding of its function, in order to change it!
- Humans, especially children, are VERY clever at getting their needs met. Often in misguided (non-relational) ways so we can model and teach them more helpful ways to get their needs met
- All behavior is acquired through conditioning, and our responses to our environment shapes our actions. Hey trauma! What's up socialization!
- Behavior is learned and taught, so can be unlearned and retaught to be more relational.

Here are some common examples of misguided behaviors, or things we say and do conflicting with our physical and mental well-being.

- Gossipping about colleagues: Possible needs: attention; Possible lagging skill/s: boundaries around what is ours to share and not ours to share, connecting with others in kinder, more interesting ways
- Not moving our bodies: Possible needs: escape, sensory input/output; Possible lagging skill/s: discipline, healthy habits, self-love, emotion regulation
- Excessive drinking and/or substance use: Possible needs: escape, attention, sensory; Possible lagging skill/s: healthy coping strategies, social skills
- Yelling at your kids: Possible needs: attention, escape; Possible lagging skill/s: self-regulation, structure and routines, ways to navigate challenging behavior that aren't punishing, but provide instruction instead
- Spending a lot of free time on screens: Possible needs: escape, attention, sensory; Possible lagging skill/s: healthy coping strategies, interpersonal skills to connect outside a screen
- Ignoring basic needs, like good sleep and healthy food: Possible need: escape, access to a preferred activity; Possible lagging skill/s: healthy habits, boundary-setting, self-love
- Ignoring our need for self-care in other ways (same as above!)

Putting It Into Practice

Misguided behavior moving us away from healthy relationships and overall wellness happens a lot amongst adults. Not to be dismayed! Here are a few strategies for shifting misguided behavior:

- **Become more aware** of how your behavior impacts your well-being or contributes to the lack thereof!
- **Identify a behavior you'd like to shift.** Think low burden (start small!) so you can practice and experiment with the concepts in this section. Need to drink more water? Follow through on a task? Pay more attention while driving by avoiding distractions?
- **Get curious.** Become a behavior detective and decode what need/s the misguided behavior is trying to communicate to you and/or what skill/s can be developed to move the needle of your behavior towards wellness.
- **Identify 1-3 things you could think, say and do differently** to support the behavior change? Think about adding structures like alerts, post-it notes with encouragement to shift or accountability partners (a safe person to tell your goal to so they can support you). What could be a thought triangle you create and practice so your brain gets clear instructions about what you WANT instead of what you DON'T WANT?
- **Practice behavior activation.** Say and do the thing even if you don't feel like it. More often than not, feelings we want more come DURING or AFTER we say and do the thing. For example, if you chose drinking more water as a behavior you'd like to have, get

yourself a good-sized water bottle and fill it the night before. The next day, grab it out of the fridge and have a calendar alert set up to ping you every hour to take ten sips or three big gulps of water, even if you're not dying of thirst. After a few weeks, you won't be able to do without drinking water, and you might experience better digestion, less fatigue and your skin might be less itchy and dry. Look at that! You did the thing!

Wrap It Up Already

Okay my loves! Lots to digest in this chapter, and you might be wondering why I'm still talking to JUST YOU when you bought this book to learn more about joy and connection in RELATIONSHIPS. Hang in there with me. Remember, the quality of our relationships has so much to do with our individual well-being, so building a solid foundation will pave the way for healthier, more joyful relationships. In the next chapter, you'll learn how to practice your superpowers, allowing you to choose the track running in the background of your life instead of what someone else chose. If you haven't already figured it out, you're magic! I can't wait to see how you use it for good for yourself and others.

<h2 style="text-align:center">Self-Reflection</h2>

- What has your family/race/culture modeled and taught you regarding how to navigate uncomfortable feelings, unhelpful thoughts and what other people say and do?
- What takeaways do you have from the chapter? Were you aware you have so much choice, with some focused attention and skill, to shift what you think, say and do?
- What song lyrics from *My Future* by Billie Eilish do you think fit this chapter and why? Message me on social media and I'll select my three favorite responses to win a signed copy of the book!

<h2 style="text-align:center">Affirmations</h2>

- I'm magic! I choose my thoughts and when I practice kinder, more helpful ones, I feel, say and do better.
- I can't wait to see the difference in how I feel in six months or a year! I'm on the path to more joy and connection already.
- When practicing gets difficult, I can say compassionate things to myself to love myself forward. I won't give up on myself!

<h2 style="text-align:center">Dive Deeper Resources</h2>

CHAPTER 4

Shifting What We Think, Feel, Say and Do

Listen to Do You Believe In Magic
by The Lovin' Spoonful

Now that you understand each point of the triangle more clearly, let's get into how to shift points to be more helpful. When we rework a triangle we don't need to make it all rainbows and unicorns. We don't need to say things like, "Everything is awesome!" or other invalidating thoughts like, "Suck it up buttercup and deal with it." We absolutely need to normalize and reality check our experiences AND we can choose to introduce different and more helpful thoughts. Think REALISTIC and HOPEFUL as a framework for creating helpful thought triangles. Here we go, with the unhelpful triangles I identified in the last chapter.

Reworking Thought Triangles

Initial Thought: I need connection but my partner is ignoring me. I keep trying to get their attention and they're not noticing. They don't care about me.

Feelings: Defeat, frustration, anger, betrayal, shame, rejection, sadness

Behavior: I withdraw, I make a passive aggressive comment, I ignore them too or, because I have an ambivalent attachment style and I might be triggered, I pester them for attention/connection.

Steps for Reworking An Unhelpful Thought Triangle

- **First,** notice an unhelpful thought or uncomfortable feeling (we want to catch ourselves before we move into saying and doing as much as possible!) and take the opportunity to change it.

- **Next,** pause for a moment, take some deep breaths and consider the wiring you're intentionally creating to override the existing wiring.

- **Lastly,** use the word <u>and</u> not *but* in your REALISTIC AND HOPEFUL reworked thought triangle. The word *but* can be activating to our systems because it can be invalidating or dismissive of what we feel. The word <u>and</u> validates our experience and redirects us in a more hopeful, chosen direction. Below is the new thought triangle I land on, completely changing the experience in my body and in my relationship.

Reworked Thought: I want to connect with my partner and I need to ask them if they have the capacity to connect right now. If not, I can handle it and take care of my own needs, or reach out to someone else.

Feelings: Calm, a little anxious to voice my needs (I'm practicing this!), hopeful, patient, empowered and grounded

Behavior: I ask if they have capacity to connect for a few minutes and they say they'd love to in ten minutes. They need to finish a task they're in the middle of. I use healthy coping strategies (more on this in a bit) to keep my nervous systems calm and open to connection.

Night and day, right? In the initial scenario, if I hadn't noticed my thoughts and feelings and had just moved into behavior patterns occurring when I'm in my head and feeling spaces, we most likely would be bickering instead of connecting. My lack of self-awareness would lead to childlike behavior, because some of my parts will go after whatever kind of attention they can get, as they are just trying to get their needs met. My practice of tuning into my self-talk and feelings is paying off because I'm getting more of my needs met, staying in connection with my partner, reducing friction in the house and my nervous system is much happier. Here are the final two reworked triangles from the previous chapter.

Initial Thought: My workplace is toxic but I can't look for anything else because I don't have the experience other people do.

Feelings: Defeat, despair, hopelessness, powerlessness, resignation, feeling trapped

Behavior: I stay in a job that harms my mental and physical health, I complain all the time to anyone who will listen, I have a hard time being productive at work, I'm so exhausted after work I hardly have a social life.

Reworked Thought: I'm struggling at work and I want to believe in possibility. I'm going to consider my options and figure something out.

Feelings: Hopeful, intrigued, curious, self-trusting, nervited (nervous/excited)

Behavior: I decide to focus on what I can do at work to further my experience, I practice my Feel Good Plan (we will get to this in the next chapter!) and work on filling my bucket to protect what well-being I have. I complain less and my work relationships improve.

Initial Thought: I can't make healthier choices. Every time I try, I fail.

Feelings: Powerlessness, stuck, sad, angry, stupid, embarrassed

Behavior: I give up, don't bother trying, I judge or envy other people.

Reworked Thought: Making healthy choices feels hard sometimes and I will keep trying. I'll figure this out by asking for help and taking care of the feelings getting in the way of making healthy choices.

Feelings: Less of what I felt before and more hopeful, connected, grounded, calm, curious

Behavior: I get curious and reach out to a health coach, I happen across a book containing just the information I need, I start practicing dropping into my body more and paying attention to its signals, I move and eat more mindfully and I find a new doctor who actually takes time to listen to me and give me new information.

Not terribly mind blowing right? Or is it? Have you truly considered or experienced how quickly we can change how we feel and what we say and do just by shifting what we think? The change can happen in minutes, sometimes less! It feels magical and it's absolutely possible for EVERYONE. Even for the most staunch grumbler or pessimist. The one spark needed to light this flame is the choice to believe in the possibilities for yourself. A bit of desire, if you will, to shift your felt experience to a better place.

Now, sometimes unhelpful behaviors come first, meaning we react by saying and doing things creating disconnection and uncomfortable thoughts and feelings. If this is the case, you may need to make a repair or have a do-over to get back to connection. We will talk more about these strategies in later chapters. And yes, we will need a whole chapter on repairing relationships!

You are empowered to choose what you think, feel, say and do most of the time. At least you are when you increase your self-awareness enough to notice when something shows up you don't want in your brain and body space. In general, this is about as much as we have control of in our lives. If we practice mastering our thoughts, if we say and do things that are good for us even if we don't FEEL like it, then we will have the ability to feel good more often, which is the goal. All feelings are part of the human experience and we can all stand to feel more comfortable feelings more of the time.

Sometimes thought triangles take time to feel resolved. We don't want to move too far away from uncomfortable feelings because they deserve space and a voice too. Uncomfortable feelings can teach us a lot about ourselves and how we are living our lives. But we don't want to live our lives at the whim of every feeling that shows up, we simply want to notice them and get curious. Practicing thought triangles can increase our self-awareness and help us manage emotional components of our experiences, as well as change our behavior to be more aligned with who and what we want to be. Which I imagine, for most, is to be more loving and more compassionate to ourselves and others.

In the beginning of this chapter, I suggested you write down thought triangles. Over time, you can simply ask yourself the question, "What is my thought triangle and how can it be more helpful for me?" when you are experiencing uncomfortable stories originating from old wiring. We absolutely can, with some practice, shift on the fly from unhelpful self-talk (thoughts) to more helpful narratives. This can be an effortful practice in the beginning and it's worth the effort. With time and practice you will notice much kinder narratives rolling around in your brain. I've witnessed this time and time again within myself, in my therapy practice and in other spaces. I believe anyone is capable of changing the stories they tell themselves. ANYONE! This means you.

Let's talk a bit more about those nervous systems I keep mentioning because our thought triangles impact our nervous systems and vice versa.There are many divisions of the nervous system, so what I write below is greatly simplified. Here are details on two nervous systems I will refer to in this book.

Parasympathetic Nervous System: Otherwise known as the "rest and digest" nervous system, responsible for initiating calm in the body, greatly impacted by stress and trauma (meaning it may not switch on as often as would be beneficial).

Sympathetic Nervous System: Otherwise known as the "fight, flight, freeze or fawn" system, when it perceives a threat, tells the body to get ready for mental and physical activity.

I'll venture a guess most humans live way more in their sympathetic nervous system responses than in their parasympathetic nervous system responses, which can cause a good amount of wear and tear on our brains and bodies. My hope is as you continue to develop your Social and Emotional Fluency, you will learn how to initiate the parasympathetic response more often. It's one of the yummiest experiences your body can experience and we need more and more of it!

Our nervous systems only have so much capacity to navigate life, also known as the window of tolerance, and each of us have a unique capacity. As many people as there are in the world, that's how many different nervous systems there are, and therefore how many different capacities exist. Whatever your capacity is, it's true and right for you AND we can increase our capacity to experience life in calm, confident and capable ways by healing wounds and growing our social and emotional skills.

The <u>window of tolerance</u> is a concept originally developed by Dr. Dan Siegel, MD to describe the optimal zone in which our bodies operate best. When a person is operating within this zone or window, they can manage, cope and process emotions and everyday life. For clients who have experienced trauma, emotion regulation can be difficult, and their window of tolerance can be quite narrow. Defenses come up, and the capacity to navigate sometimes even the tiniest of stressors becomes less and less. This can be because unprocessed experiences and emotions essentially build up on our nervous systems, taking up space so to speak, and the build up can lead to overwhelming feelings pushing us outside our window of tolerance.

The good news is this is not a fixed trajectory. Healing our brains and bodies, and building the skills to process and navigate life experiences, slowly but surely expands our window of tolerance. You are learning how to do this just by practicing more helpful thought triangles, including how we think about stress. What we know about stress is that how often we experience it, in what intensity and how we think about it all factor into whether or not it has a negative impact on us. You can dig into research on this in the Dive Deeper resources at the end of this chapter, but for the purpose of practicing thought triangles, I'll share an unhelpful triangle and then rework it. You may want to copy this one down and practice it yourself because, like you've already witnessed, shifting what we think, say and do has a big impact on how we feel. And how we feel impacts pretty much everything else! Here is the unhelpful triangle and the rework.

Initial Thought: I can't be everything to everyone. I'm drowning in work and home stuff. There's no end in sight.

Feelings: Despair, frustration, rage, overwhelm, STRESS, inadequacy, helplessness

Behavior: I chug Coke Zeros and coffee like they're going out of style, I drop workouts to focus on work tasks, I snap at anyone within earshot, I isolate from friends, I zone out on social while sitting on the toilet until my legs go numb trying to capture any moment to myself (this one is too accurate right?)

Reworked Thought: I'm beyond overwhelmed. I can tell my boundaries have slipped and I can make more compassionate decisions to shift back to being well.

Feelings: Hopeful, tired, stressed (but less so), overwhelmed (but less so), frustration (but less so), compassionate, more gentle with myself

Behavior: I sit down and make a list of shifts I can make over time to protect and foster my well-being, adding workouts back in, chill with the caffeine intake, prioritize going to bed even 30 minutes earlier, set calendar reminders to practice more helpful self-talk and feelings check-ins, set a boundary at work about how much I can and will take on.

Sometimes we get a little, or a lot, off track. Life comes at us hot and heavy sometimes, and when our skill set is fragile and/or we have so much on our plates, we can get a bit wobbly in our social and emotional skills practice. Thought triangles and other strategies can go a long way towards helping us get back on track and expanding our window of tolerance. The tools and strategies I teach in this book can move us back more quickly into our window of tolerance where we feel more open, curious, calm, present and safe.

Self-Reflection

- What are ways you can remind yourself to pause throughout the day, notice your inner dialogue and practice thought triangles? Keep in mind REALISTIC and HOPEFUL. Use the word AND, because the word teaches our brains to hold space for the whole human experience.
- What lyrics from *Do You Believe In Magic* by The Lovin' Spoonful do you think fit this chapter and why? Message me on social media and I'll select my three favorite responses to win a signed copy of the book!

Affirmations

- Creating new thoughts and practicing different behaviors means I'm changing how I feel. Little by little, I can feel better more often.

Dive Deeper Resources

CHAPTER 5

The Most Important
Life Skill You Didn't Learn

Listen to Check Yo Self *by Ice Cube*

How many of you were taught the steps to tie your shoelaces as a child? Taught the steps for riding a bike (bum on seat, hands on handlebars, keep your head up)? Taught how to drive a car or manage a bank account or bake a cake? These are life skills many of us were taught, and I imagine those skills have come in handy for most over the years. But there is a life skill many of us missed learning, mostly because our caregivers didn't know how to practice the skill either! I'm talking about the steps to process uncomfortable emotions in healthy ways. Sure, we've learned how to navigate feelings in ways anywhere from helpful to unhelpful, even harmful, but most are not super supportive of our well-being and certainly not for the well-being of our relationships.

Remember, our younger selves were very clever and did their best to manage discomfort (or worse), but many of us are still navigating feelings in childlike ways because we don't know how to do it differently, or better. Kids, teens and adults are numbing, distracting, stuffing down, compartmentalizing and dissociating from their feelings, a lot of which happens because we just don't know what else to do and/or haven't developed new strategies to replace old. If we don't practice kinder, more compassionate ways to soothe our nervous systems, if we don't extract information our feelings are sending our way to guide us through life and if we don't stay in connection with ourselves and others while we are doing this, we can cause a lot of hurt to ourselves and others. A LOT.

Trigger Warning: Mentions of unaliving ideation or attempts and self-harm are mentioned in this section. I don't go into detail, but you should check in with yourself before reading the following paragraph. Otherwise, skip ahead!

We know enough at this moment in time about how certain behaviors and thoughts impact not only our mental health, but also our physical health. We are a society full of unhelpful, even harmful, coping strategies for a variety of reasons. And while some coping strategies are normalized (shopping, drinking alcohol, using other substances, binge watching shows, gaming for hours) and, if used in moderation, aren't problems in and of themselves, there are a few coping strategies still being stigmatized and misunderstood. Suicide ideation and suicide attempts are ways to escape. Self-harm can be a distraction from other pain, a way to feel SOMETHING, a much needed adrenaline rush and more. These practices are meeting needs (see the last chapter on functions of behavior), and until we have the skill, will and capacity to develop more loving strategies to meet those needs, humans will continue to turn to them. We shouldn't be in the don't do that business. We want to focus on the *what's a healthier, kinder strategy I can replace it with business.*

Some of the coping strategies I mentioned (gaming, shows, substances, food) are not in and of themselves unhelpful. What we want to consider is am I making connections and wiring in my brain in harmful ways? Am I teaching my nervous systems that when I'm uncomfortable, turning to a glass of wine or online shopping is the way I manage the feels? This is a neural pathway we want to disrupt and reroute, or avoid creating all together. Before we get into the steps for processing emotions in healthy ways (don't worry, there are only three steps!), let's get into the parts of the brain involved in self-management. I'm providing a really simplistic overview of certain parts of the brain, so if you're interested in diving deeper, use the QR Code at the end of this chapter.

The Amygdala, Our Security Guard and Emotions Alarm

The amygdala are an almond-shaped parts of the brain sitting slightly behind both of your ears. The amygdala are part of the limbic system, or the feelings part of the brain. The amygdala regulates breathing, your heart rate and blood pressure, all things autonomic, meaning we don't have to consciously think about them. The amygdala are also our security guards. If I'm walking down my street at night and hear a rustling in the bushes, I want my amygdala to leap into action so I can fight, flight, freeze or fawn. Fight and freeze mean the obvious, flight indicates the instinct to run away and fawn indicates the desire to befriend the threat in some way, meaning what we say and do may look like we are okay with what is happening but WE ARE NOT. These are all automatic reactions we can't control, and we do not choose them. The amygdala react, they don't think at all.

The problem with the amygdala is they can get wired to not only jump into action and react when met with an actual physical threat, they can also get trained to react to a perceived threat. This can be tricky because our perceptions might have us freaking out over a difficult work email, a partner forgetting to pick up their stuff for the umpteenth time or a kiddo refusing to put on their jacket when it's snowing outside. We want to avoid saying and doing from the amygdala because we will most likely say and do something not in alignment with who we are or who we want to be.

So, when the amygdala experiences a threat (or the perception of one), they send an alarm through the rest of the body and the nervous systems get engaged. Stress hormones, like adrenaline and cortisol, bathe the brain and body so they can be ready for survival. This is a healthy and necessary response SOME OF THE TIME. If these reactions of stress hormones happen frequently, and the individual doesn't have the capacity to deal with the experience, then the brain and body can start to be on constant high alert. Many victims of trauma feel shame and self-loathing because they didn't fight or run away, instead they may have frozen or fawned, and it may have looked and felt like they were okay with what was happening. If this is the case for you, know your brain and body did its job, they kept you alive. And now you have the opportunity to release the shame and move forward, because this burden isn't yours to carry anymore. It never was, and now you can lay it down with the help of some intentional healing and growing work!

The Hippocampus, Our Memory Keeper

The hippocampi, also a part of the limbic system, are adjacent to our amygdala and are our memory savers. The hippocampi store old patterns, old experiences and old perceptions. When we are repeatedly exposed to trauma and stress as children, our amygdala is activated, and the constant activation of the amygdala causes the hippocampus to underdevelop, making it more difficult for some individuals to recall needed information, memories and more. The hippocampus also dramatically influences how and when our amygdala reacts, because it has all the information of those early experiences stored, and feeds the amygdala and other parts of the brain the stored information.

Keep in mind too, there is research showing we usually don't remember events and experiences as they factually happened, we instead remember how we interpreted events at the time they occurred. This can be problematic, since our interpretations often come from a subjective, emotional and childlike space. Again, these memories are valid AND we want to regularly evaluate them to see if we can heal from them and move on through growing.

The Cortex, Our Thinking Brain

The last part of the brain I'll mention here is the cortex, specifically the prefrontal cortex and neocortex. The neocortex is actually part of the limbic system (or feeling brain) as well, but it's the part we want to be engaged in more often. Sensory function, language, motor function and conscious thought are all in the neocortex. The prefrontal cortex, which makes up about a third of the neocortex, is where our executive functioning is performed, our logic and higher reasoning, decision-making, time management, organization, thoughtful social behavior and even the expression of our personality. Another major function of the prefrontal cortex is to regulate emotions and that, my friends, is why we want to engage it more often instead of saying and doing from our amygdalas. Along with the hippocampi, the prefrontal cortex can be underdeveloped in brains that experienced toxic stress and/or trauma, the impact of which mimic the symptoms of Attention Deficit Hyperactivity Disorder (ADHD) and Attention Deficit Disorder (ADD). This is indicated in research showing children who are in foster care (due to trauma and/or further causing trauma) have a disproportionately high rate of ADHD and ADD diagnoses. We want to consider, based on solid assessments and evaluations, is it ADHD/ADD and/or is it trauma, and how might we change treatment one way or the other?

When we are operating within our window of tolerance, the cortex, hippocampi and amygdala are all communicating with each other beautifully. When the amygdala is activated, it shuts off communication to the other parts of the brain and moves into react mode. If our nervous systems are wired to perceive threats around every corner, or certain corners even when we are physically safe, we want to find ways that work for us to soothe the amygdala and teach it to only show up when it really matters, in times of true threat. The benefits of doing so include lowering the allostatic load, or wear and tear on our nervous systems from constant amygdala activation, which can lead to burnout and worse. We can then increase our capacity to experience more feel good chemicals (dopamine, serotonin, oxytocin) and access parts of our brain facilitating more calm and connection. We can receive these benefits by overriding our programming with some low burden tools, accessible even when we are in distress. This can take time for those of us whose nervous systems are reactionary. Be patient with yourself, take deep breaths and pause often. In the next chapter, we will dive into steps for soothing your nervous systems you get to put your own spin on. You will practice discovering your secret sauce for feeling good, most of the time. Not all the time! But definitely more often.

Being in Relationship With Others is Triggering

An often harmful component of relationships is we can operate within them from our wounds and from reactionary wiring. Each of us, in some capacity or other, has relational wounds, even if those wounds wouldn't be categorized as trauma. Remember, trauma most often happens in relationships, and the residue of those experiences can become the wounds I'm referring to. We often attract partners from our wounded parts, re-enacting our hard experiences until we heal those parts, those wounds. We can also be triggered by sights, smells, certain songs, places, experiences and more having nothing to do with our current partner or friend, but our nervous systems don't always understand this. Why the hell would we want to even attempt relationships then, if a big part of what we experience in them can be tender, raw and even painful? Because what gets hurt or traumatized in relationships needs to be healed both individually AND in relationship. We need to have corrective experiences by showing up for ourselves, and having folks show up for us in different and better ways, so we can begin to heal wounds plaguing our well-being and relationships.

We will dive into this later in the book, but here is something to take in right now. It's not anyone else's job to manage our triggers AND those of us who are triggered to be clingy, intensely co-dependent or fiercely independent, often because we didn't have emotionally mature caregivers as children, can ask safe partners or friends for support. If you tend to look outside of yourself for help with regulation, then I encourage you to develop the skills to manage your triggers and self-regulate so you can foster self-trust.

What Exactly is a Trigger?

A trigger is a reaction in our bodies alerting us to the wounds we carry. Triggers are invitations to bring the unconscious to consciousness AND they are very uncomfortable experiences for our bodies. We need the skills to heal them. Why? Because a trigger is an opportunity to understand how we suffer, so we can learn how to ease the suffering. Remember, it's not someone else's job to heal your triggers or to not trigger you, but they can help! They can be bonus support.

When we are triggered, we move into the Dorsal Vagal State, the Fight, Flight, Freeze or Fawn response. This book, and other resources I provide, can help guide your nervous systems towards the Ventral Vagal State (see the Dive Deeper Resources for more on vagal states), which means you can move through life from a place of openness, curiosity, compassion and mindfulness more often. You're operating within your window of tolerance. All of our nervous systems need a little, or a lot, more of this. Do you imagine this as a possibility for you? Remember we are meant to have ALL the feelings, but it doesn't mean we want those feelings to overwhelm our systems so much that we say and do disconnecting things. We can still train our nervous systems to experience calm more often.

Let's say an experience occurs your nervous systems perceive as unsafe or a threat. Here are two ways we don't want to navigate a trigger.

Your avoidant (remember, this means you move away from opportunities for support) wiring, parts and attachment style communicates you can't trust anyone and no one can help you. This can all occur subconsciously. A reminder from Chapter Two is we often get triggered into an insecurely attached state. Notice I'm weaving together some threads here of concepts you've already learned about in earlier chapters.

You isolate, potentially turning to unhelpful coping strategies encouraging numbing out (sex, substances), distracting (binge watching shows, scrolling social media, video games), stuffing down of emotions (eating too much or too little, gaslighting yourself) and essentially reinforcing experiences of loneliness and even despair.

In order for us to teach our nervous systems how to experience more calm, more often, we need to practice Steps for Healthy Emotion Processing. At this point in time, we have enough research to back up the claim that processing emotions in healthy ways increases our quality of life. Our mental and physical health improves and relationships have more possibilities to thrive. Processing emotions in healthy ways is simple, yet not always easy. Until it is! The more we practice these steps, the more we unlearn unhelpful (even harmful) ways of managing uncomfortable feelings and the easier it gets.

Now say the same experience as above occurs, and your nervous systems perceive something as unsafe or a threat. Here are some **steps for processing emotions** and triggers in a healthy way.

Pause, Breathe: This first step can be the hardest! Many of us are wired to react quickly and in certain ways to uncomfortable feelings. To disrupt those patterns, we need to invite the pause. When I pause, I'm taking deep breaths to get as much oxygen to my brain as possible, and to let my brain and body just take a beat.

Connect with Feelings: Identifying uncomfortable feelings as accurately as you can, which lets your brain know you're picking up what it's putting down. Feelings are just information (you learned this in Chapter Two) from the brain. What increases our discomfort is the meaning we imprint on the feelings. All feelings are okay, what matters most is what we say and do with the feelings. A great tool for this practice is a feelings chart or wheel (use the QR code at the end of this chapter for links).

Love Note: Teeny, tiny shifts towards feeling our feelings are so, so important! The self-trust and wisdom we gain from this practice is a gamechanger in the way we move through life. Trust me on this one! Please don't skip over these smaller, yet significant strategies like connecting with feelings. All of these strategies build on each other to create a powerful social and emotional toolkit. You are an adult now, with tools and strategies in front of you to feel the feels. You will be okay! More than okay.

Soothe Your Nervous Systems with a Feel Good Plan: We aren't meant to feel good all of the time but could we feel better more often? Absolutely. If I identify having anxiety at an eight on a scale of 1-10, I will want to take care of my nervous systems with healthy coping strategies before I do anything else, and I can do this with a Feel Good Plan.

A Feel Good Plan (I came up with this name when I worked as an elementary school counselor) is a list of things we can think, say and do to take care of our brain and bodies. This tool might seem simple and silly, but having a visual to consistently remind our brains we want to process feelings in more healthy and helpful ways is just a brain hack. It makes the process of disrupting old patterns much easier. There are three things everyone should have on their Feel Good Plan (and I don't should on you very often!).

Movement: Our bodies, in ways unique to our abilities, are wired to experience movement, and a lack thereof can lead to trapped energy in our bodies. Movement is the number one evidence-based therapeutic intervention for managing anxiety and depression. We know so much about how movement improves and supports mental, emotional and physical well-being, so put a kind of movement you enjoy on your Feel Good Plan. Remember you may not feel like practicing a lot of the tools and strategies in this book IN THE MOMENT, but the feelings you are seeking most likely will come AFTER saying or doing the thing. Hula hoop, dance in your kitchen, walk with a friend, throw some weights around or shake it out, you have so many choices!

Helpful Self-Talk: Say I had a stressful day and chose to take a walk from my Feel Good Plan, but the whole time I was walking my self-talk was shaming, blaming and pissy. How less intensely do you think I'd be feeling those uncomfortable feelings? Yeah, not so much! We want to engage with realistic and hopeful self-talk (or thoughts) you learned about in Chapter Four. All you need here is your thought triangle tool to practice this one!

Breath Practice: When I'm stressed, I hold my breath and I know I'm not alone! I often remind clients to take a breath in session when they are experiencing uncomfortable feelings in their bodies. There are a bunch of different breath practices, and just like movement, I encourage you to find one suiting you. Breath practices can be uncomfortable at first so go gently with them! Here are a few ideas.

- *Polyvagal Breathing:* Breathe in for four counts then out for eight counts. This type of breathing stimulates the vagus nerve, which is responsible for initiating calm down response in our nervous systems. Repeat until you experience a change.

- *Box or Square Breathing:* Inhale and exhale for the same amount of counts. For example, exhale all of your breath, then inhale for four counts, hold at the top of the breath for four counts, exhale for four counts, hold at the bottom of the breath for four counts, and repeat. You can use your finger to trace a square in the space in front of you. Repeat until you experience a change.

- *Hot Chocolate Breathing:* This is a great practice for those who work with kids in any capacity because it engages different senses and can be very calming. Picture yourself holding a mug of hot chocolate (or coffee or bowl of soup) and inhale while imagining the smell of the chocolate, then exhale as if you are blowing on it to cool it down. Repeat until you experience a change.

Other practices on a Feel Good Plan include strategies grounding you in your body, such as naming one thing you see, hear, feel, taste or smell, using objects to connect to (I often use crystals or rocks) and butterfly hugs. More on these in the Dive Deeper Resources at the end of this chapter. **Finally, there are two things I suggest NO ONE has on their plan.**

Vices: We've already discussed how our brains and bodies learn all kinds of coping strategies, some helpful and other less so. Many of the less so strategies fall under the vice umbrella when accessed excessively, such as shopping, gambling, food and certain substances. Please do not put vice strategies on the list of ways to calm your nervous systems. They provide only a short-term hil of feel good chemicals, and the consequences can be very harmful to our well-being and relationships.

Screens: I know this is going to be a tricky one for most, but screens provide a false sense of calm. They don't actually help us process uncomfortable feelings, but can trap them instead. I'm all for binge-watching your favorite show or scrolling social, but I recommend not doing these when you're feeling uncomfortable. First use other Feel Good Plan strategies to lower the intensity of discomfort, THEN move to screens if you'd like. This way you won't be reinforcing neural connection between feeling uncomfortable and reaching for a screen. Exceptions to this might be using an app providing emotional regulation support or a video with a breathing technique. However, if you get distracted easily when on your phone, pick a different strategy.

You can find more information about these processes and steps, including Feel Good Plan examples, on my website and through the Dive Deeper Resources QR code at the end of this chapter.

In addition to the things mentioned above everyone should have on their Feel Good Plan, minus the two categories I invite you to exclude, you can put ANYTHING you'd like on your plan. Snuggle your guinea pig, crinkle dried leaves in your hands, water your plants, stick your head out a window to catch some fresh air, rub or tickle your arms gently (I do this when I can't sleep), write a letter to your future self, go to your favorite bench in the park near your home, pray, talk to a trusted friend or schedule a therapy session. You get the idea! Connect with things you can think, say or do representing YOU and all those things making you who you are.

Once you've moved through the process, and have hopefully lowered the intensity of your uncomfortable feelings a few notches, you should then be in a more regulated place from which to navigate whatever experience brought on the discomfort in the first place. This process for being with our feelings and taking care of our brains and bodies is, let's say, an undergraduate level of processing feelings. In the next section, we're going to get a master's degree in navigating feelings! I highly recommend you stick with the undergraduate level of processing until you notice new wiring being created on a regular basis. The skills of pausing, identifying feelings and soothing your nervous systems are foundational to getting a master's degree in healthy emotional processing!

Something to consider, I have consulted with hundreds, if not thousands, of adults through my work with school districts and buildings, parent organizations and parents in my online space, and practicing the Steps for Healthy Emotional Processing, including Feel Good Plans, is a tried and true strategy! In fact, a large school district south of Seattle implemented Feel Good Plans district-wide for its educators, parents and students. To this day, I still get feedback from adults in those spaces on how this simple strategy has changed the way they manage their classrooms, connect with the unique nervous systems of their students (and staff) and increase everyone's capacity to engage and learn. If you are a parent and/or work with children in any capacity, I highly recommend everyone create a Feel Good Plan. Here's how using a Feel Good Plan can look like in action while navigating a trigger. Again, an experience occurs your nervous systems perceive as unsafe or a threat.

Your avoidant (remember, this means you move away from opportunities for support) wiring, parts and attachment style communicates you can't trust anyone and no one can help you.

This can all occur subconsciously.

You isolate, potentially turning to unhelpful coping strategies encouraging numbing out (sex, substances), distracting (binge watching shows, scrolling social media, video games), stuffing down of emotions (eating too much or too little, gaslighting yourself) and essentially reinforcing experiences of loneliness and even despair.

What we want to practice instead, when an experience occurs your nervous system perceives as unsafe or a threat, is something like this.

Your avoidant (remember, this means you move away from opportunities for support) wiring, parts and attachment style communicates you can't trust anyone and no one can help you. You are developing self-awareness, so what used to happen subconsciously, you now bring to your awareness. You know it's there. So you pause, identify the feelings you're experiencing and then do the following:

DISRUPT the pattern. Choose something from your Feel Good Plan such as breathing. Place your hand on your belly or heart and say out loud or in your head, "I'm safe, I can calm down, I can ask for a hug." You pause the interaction until your nervous systems are more calm and your thinking brain is back online. This may take seconds or minutes, or it may take much longer in the beginning of your work.

You make a request for the kind of support you'd like. A request is different from a demand. Requests are just requests, or asks not needing a certain outcome and ones easily fulfilled by you or someone else if the other person doesn't have the skill/capacity to give you what you need. A demand has an expectation of an outcome and comes with negative consequences if not met. Often REALLY negative consequences.

Master's Level Emotional Processing

"All feelings are okay, what matters most is what we say and do with them" is a phrase I share often with parents I'm coaching privately, with parents I'm coaching in the SHIFT Online Community as well as with therapy clients. Try telling this to nervous systems doing ANYTHING BUT being okay with what we are feeling. Oof. Our minds are so complex and have so many learned, but unhelpful, ways of navigating uncomfortable feelings as adults. Helpful as kids, when we had fewer options for coping, but most of us don't want to be managing big, uncomfortable feelings in the same ways we did as kids! But we do just this, often. A few reminders about feelings below.

- Feelings themselves are not unbearable. It's often the meaning we assign to feelings that is unbearable.
- Feelings are just information from our brains and can be really helpful in guiding us, if we can manage the feelings in helpful ways.
- Feelings help us connect to our truest selves, and to others. It is so necessary for our well-being to learn to be with feelings, even the tricky ones.

In the last section, I focused on simple things we can do to process uncomfortable feelings in healthy and compassionate ways, by pausing, checking in with our feelings and using Feel Good Plans. I hope you've been practicing! Once we feel more competent with the foundational steps to processing emotions in healthy ways, we can graduate to the masters' level of emotion processing. We are much more likely to experience deeper connections to ourselves and others when we practice graduate course processes of being with uncomfortable feelings like disgust, rage, horror, shame and grief. So how do we work our way through graduate school (maybe even PhD level!) processing of feelings? Well, we bring our feelings closer and closer to us. Let me share an experience (vulnerability at a 10 here folks) of when I DID NOT process my emotions well, and what I am practicing differently now.

A few years ago, in the fall of 2020, I was in a very rough space in my life. The pandemic was in full swing and I had major life transitions and relational disruptions happening (including a separation from my husband). I was also experiencing burnout in my therapy practice. Then, I said something really not okay to a friend. Pause with me here for a moment. None of the reasons above, all of which were activating the state of my nervous systems, justified me causing hurt or harm. Despite what we are experiencing, we cannot make excuses for our behavior. We are 100% accountable for any hurt we cause others NO MATTER WHAT. My purpose in sharing what I was navigating is illustrative of me acknowledging and taking accountability for the interaction with my friend. I can have compassion for myself, for everything I was navigating, and still own what I said was not okay.

I made a major relational mistake. These things happen because we are human, but instead of paying attention to the harm I had done, I dug in and continued to interact with this person in a triggered state. I was in my amygdala big time for all the reasons I've written about and because of how I felt about my mistake. Eventually, there were some attempts to make a repair, but I couldn't fully grasp the impact of my behavior at the time, so the attempts didn't land well. More on making repairs in later chapters.

Friends, my brain was doing ALL THE THINGS to distract me from feelings of shame, disgust and horror I was experiencing because of what I had said. I was focusing on my friend's reaction, blaming them for things they said back to me, and on the challenging things taking place in my life. I was focusing on anything BUT being with the feelings themselves. If I'd have had the awareness and ability to be with my discomfort, I could have used the processes and tools I've discussed in this book instead.

- **Paused and identified my feelings** of disgust, shame and horror for what they were.

- **Chosen something from my Feel Good Plan** to settle my nervous systems, even just a little bit. The next two steps are where we get into the graduate school of emotional processing.

- I could have then **followed the emotional threads** of disgust, shame and horror and connected those feelings to early childhood experiences where my younger selves got stuck carrying emotional burdens. I've been practicing this recently, years too late after I said the thing to my friend. With some moments of mindfulness, I have been able to make connections to early childhood trauma occurring at certain ages, mostly as a toddler, but also as a teen.

- Next, I'd have **spent some time in my mind with those little versions of myself.** I recently had an internal dialogue with them going something like, "Hey babes (what I call my younger selves), what's wrong? What do you need? How can I help you? Oh, I get it. Those things that happened are horrible, and what has happened feels unsafe. I hear you. I'm taking care of you now and I'm not going anywhere. Come here. You're safe." This strategy is an aspect of re-parenting younger parts of ourselves who got stuck emotionally because of trauma and other emotional wounds. Big, intense feelings are held onto by younger parts of ourselves who didn't have the wherewithal to manage the feelings. Once I've spent time soothing my little ones (think of the best teacher/coach you've ever interacted with and use their same tone and voice if you need a model for this), I notice more emotional intensity emerging along with feelings of relief and freedom, as my younger selves get to just be kids now and not have to carry big, heavy emotional burdens. Me, my adult self, is giving the younger versions of myself the care and attention they need. This is the privilege of existing in these amazing, unique and complex brains and bodies of ours. We can give ourselves what we didn't get as kiddos or young adults in healthy, compassionate ways.

- **This is a practice.** We might need to visit our younger selves several times before feelings are more manageable. As we do this, we build trust in our internal systems AND we let our brains know we don't need the distractions from feelings. We are adults now and can be with feelings safely.

If I had known what I know now about the graduate school of emotional processing, I imagine I would have been with my uncomfortable feelings and leaned into making a heartfelt, genuine repair instead of causing more harm. If you feel ready to take emotional processing to deeper levels, consider taking some time to read or listen to No Bad Parts by Richard Schwartz, where he discusses the concept of connection with our younger selves and the complexity of the mind.

Undergraduate, graduate and PhD levels of healthy emotion processing are meant to be practiced both proactively and reactively. A proactive practice can look like infusing our days with things from our Feel Good Plan and scheduling time to check-in with ourselves to see if we have feelings we need to tend to. We should be fiercely and gently protective of these practices so they don't get crowded out or dropped when we get busy. Instead, when this happens, we double down on them. A reactive practice looks just like it sounds. When we experience tricky life shit and/or our feelings are intensely uncomfortable, we should lean even more into our Feel Good Plans and create mindful moments to tend to feelings.

Squirrels

Have you seen the movie UP? With the boy named Russell, the grandpa and the floating house with balloons? If not, it's darling and I highly recommend you watch it so you can get the reference I'm making in this section. At one point in the movie, the grandpa and the boy encounter a dog who has a voice collar allowing it to communicate like a human. All the training and technology is no match for the dog's instincts, though, so when the dog is in conversation (like, really talking) with the boy and grandpa, the interactions are frequently interrupted by squirrel sightings the dog can't ignore.

Our brains are clever and parts of our brain are very instinctual (refer to the chapter on brain wiring). When we experience emotional distress, usually as children, and we don't have capable, skilled adults to help us process our distress, our brains step in to distract us with "squirrels" because we can't process our emotions on our own. Squirrels can come in the form of physical pain, excess weight, disease, perfectionism, busy-ness, social media, media in general, fixation on people and experiences (I call this spinning out) and so much more. Squirrels are an automatic coping mechanism really helping us as children, but no longer serving us as adults.

Our work as adults is to increase awareness of what our squirrels are, and then to say to our brains, "Hey brain, we don't need to do those things anymore." Then we go inward and connect with our inner emotional landscape by asking ourselves (really our younger parts), "Hey there, what is wrong? What are you feeling? What can I do to help?" Many parts of ourselves can be considered children, and need a compassionate, nurturing adult to hold space for their feelings and do what the adults in their lives couldn't do for them at the time. We can remind those parts we (the adult) are in charge and they are safe with us. When we engage in this practice, we help heal and grow our little ones, making them less likely to show up in intense, uncomfortable ways. Our squirrels should show up less and less as we experience more grounding, presence and peace in our bodies. And that, my friends, is every human's work: To get out of our heads and into our bodies more often in order to experience the fullness of what life has to offer.

As humans, we can be so disconnected from feelings and yet, it's being with feelings that provides so much wisdom and guidance and ultimately, healing and growing. Meet yourself where you are, with the emotion processing skills you have, and shift from there. You should notice, over time, more emotional stability, steadier moods, more calm and increased confidence when navigating tricky life stuff. The other side of developing better emotion processing skills is a great place to be!

Love Note: When we are on healing and growing paths, we might expect to show up perfectly because we "know better" now. We might feel guilt or shame when experiencing a trigger, or show up in ways not in alignment with our new knowledge and practices. My friends, knowing and doing are two different experiences and skill sets! It takes time to implement what we know, to put it into action, and we don't need to be perfect in this work. We should just want to become better each day as we hone our social and emotional skills. Just because a setback feels familiar, doesn't mean we are the same, and are back to square one of our journey. To help you move away from perfectionism and towards acceptance of your humanity, look for what was different or better in challenging experiences versus getting stuck in what uncomfortable feelings you felt.

Self-Reflection

- Which step of Healthy Emotion Processing do you need the most practice with?
- What squirrels can you identify in your life?
- How will you remind yourself to disrupt patterns of unhelpful coping strategies and invite new, more compassionate ones in?
- What song lyrics from *Check Yo Self* by Ice Cube do you think fit this chapter and why? Message me on social media and I'll select my three favorite responses to win a signed copy of the book!

Affirmations

- I choose to heal and grow to create safer, more joyful spaces for myself and others.
- I can grow my comfort zone by learning to be with discomfort.
- I'm good enough as I am AND I can always be learning how to be a better human. My efforts in this direction are never wasted!

Dive Deeper Resources

CHAPTER 6

Boundaries: Everyone's
Least Favorite Skill to Practice

Listen to this is how i learn to say no *by EMELINE*

When we get to know our emotional landscape and develop better skills to navigate it, we should take our knowing and put it to good use! One of the most important ways we can do this is by setting healthy boundaries. We have not been taught very well to set healthy boundaries. We do come into this world with certain boundaries. Have you ever tried to coax a baby to eat more food than they want? It's a no go. Have you seen a young child lean away from someone who wants to hold them, or have you tried to give a child a pink cup when they really want an orange one? Also a no go. Babies and toddlers will let you know what is okay or not okay for them. But over time, adults can sometimes teach children to override their innate sense of boundaries. I believe this doesn't serve children well in the long-term. As adults, we want to get back to an understanding of what our boundaries are, and then honor them. If this is an intimidating practice for you, I get it! Most likely it's hard for you because of reasons discussed earlier in the book, such as where our brain wiring comes from. Don't stress, though, healthy boundary setting is a skill you're already developing as you begin to use the tools and strategies laid out in the book so far.

What's the big deal about boundaries? Why are they so important? We need to set mental, physical, emotional and spiritual boundaries in our lives so we know what is in alignment with who we are and what isn't, what's okay and not okay for us, what is our responsibility and what is the responsibility of others. What are the yeses? The no's and the maybes? Boundaries define what is me and not me, where I end and someone else begins, and are a healthy part of our identity. If we don't know what is ours to take care of and what is not, we can experience A LOT of discomfort. We can overextend ourselves into other people's lives and create all kinds of energy leaks. Oppositely, we might under connect with people and not have enough opportunities for joy and connection to enter our lives. When we learn to set healthy boundaries, we actually experience freedom to move through life in more centered, connected and compassionate ways. We also give people we are in relationship with, whether colleagues, students, our own kids or our partners, permission to do the same. When we set healthy boundaries, we create so much room for the hell yeses in our lives!

Another benefit of practicing healthy boundary setting is to get closer and closer to the elusive thing called balance. If you picture all of the ways you expend energy as buckets in front of you, which buckets would be the most full and which buckets would be the least full? Is your work bucket overflowing but your friendship bucket half full? Is your Feel Good Plan bucket empty but the bucket representing your kids spilling out all over the place? A lack of balance in energy expenditure and overall life usually exists because we aren't setting enough self and relational boundaries. This makes a lot of sense if you think about it!

The practice of setting healthy boundaries, of which healthy emotion processing is a huge part of, can be one of the hardest skills to acquire because so much of what we experience models and teaches us the opposite. We have so many examples of people losing their shit over the tiniest things, having no idea what a boundary is, let alone how to communicate and/or respect one when it's being presented. Without good examples to give our brains direction, we often flounder until we find someone or something to guide us. I hope this book, and the additional resources going along with it, is enough guidance to get you moving along the path. I also hope that with some intention, you can find more examples of healthy boundary setting to speed up your rewiring and skill building in this area.

If healthy boundaries have so many benefits to our well-being, why are they so damn hard to set? When I've asked this question to the thousands of people who've attended my workshops, hands shoot up or the chat box pops off! We worry about not being liked, being good or kind, being rejected and/or abandoned, making someone angry, losing employment or a relationship and the list goes on and on. Setting healthy boundaries feels very high stake to most of our systems, rightly so if we are operating from parts of ourselves who are much younger. Of course, setting healthy boundaries feels difficult to our inner children because they were so enmeshed and codependent on others to keep them alive. When we are developing our boundary setting practice, it's really important to be in a calm, connected and curious state so the adult in charge (your present self) is the one establishing boundaries.

Boundaries must come from a place of love and compassion, not anger or fear. Setting healthy boundaries protects our energy, good thoughts and compassionate feelings about ourselves and others. Without boundaries, we might resent others or tend to feel more shame, guilt, frustration, self-doubt and more. These feelings definitely shift us AWAY from joy and connection. Setting healthy boundaries takes courage and lots and lots of practice. A lot a lot.

Love Note: You are a good, kind human when you set boundaries. In fact, you are a kinder, better human when you set boundaries, so rewrite your personal narrative if it tells you otherwise. Outdated narratives probably come from those who benefit or have benefitted from your lack of boundaries and that, my loves, deserves some major compassion for your younger self who sacrificed their well-being for others. No more! Your well-being is priceless and must be protected.

A Common Misunderstanding About Boundaries

Boundaries have only to do with your own thoughts, feelings and behaviors. They have nothing to do with other people's thoughts, feelings and behaviors. Often, when we begin our boundary setting journey, we practice magical thinking. We tell ourselves something like, "My boundary is my dating life won't be discussed when I go home for the holidays. I will communicate this with my parents and (here's the magical thinking) they WILL NOT bring up my dating life over the holidays." This is an expectation folks, not a boundary. When we want an outcome that sits in someone else's court, because it's their thoughts, feelings and behaviors we want to control or change, this is not a boundary. Boundaries can be set in response to how others behave, yet we can't control HOW others behave. Here's an example, see if you can notice the subtle, yet important differences between an expectation and a boundary.

Scenario: Tanisha is visiting family for the holidays.
Boundary: Tanisha is not okay with the homophobic and transphobic language her family often uses. Before the visit, Tanisha gives her mom a heads up that if conversations move in this direction, she will speak up kindly, but firmly. If the language

continues and/or her family isn't receptive or respectful, she will leave the room. As a last resort, she will end the visit early.

Expectation: Tanisha is not okay with the homophobic and transphobic language her family often uses. Before the visit, Tanisha gives her mom a heads up that if conversations move in this direction, she will speak up kindly, but firmly. When the family starts to use language she isn't comfortable with, she asks them to stop and they don't. Tanisha feels very uncomfortable, but continues the visit and the pattern of behavior continues.

What differences did you notice between an expectation and a boundary? When Tanisha sets a boundary, she clearly communicates with her mom how she will navigate any unkind interaction. Tanisha has a plan for how she will respond, and smartly recognizes she can't control the behavior of family members, only her own behavior.

If you'd like to dig further into the work of healthy boundary setting, there are several books I recommend in the Dive Deeper Resources. Practicing the tools and strategies in this book lays the groundwork for you to lean into these other books, as well as the other materials linked to in the Dive Deeper Resources. Until you have an opportunity to read these books, I'll give you a simplistic overview of healthy boundary setting and a few strategies to keep in mind, then I'll send you on your way to explore the deeper practices they present.

Making Boundary Setting as Low Burden as Possible

Let's get your brain on board with practicing healthy boundary setting by anchoring ourselves to the benefits of doing so. When your automatic brain falls back on old wiring, and tries to talk you out of practicing boundary setting, engaging your conscious mind with helpful self-talk like, "Boundary setting can be hard

AND it can get easier and easier. Healthy boundary setting is a practice and in everyone's highest good." (Repeat the mantra ten times, put it on a post-it note, do whatever you need to do). Setting healthy boundaries is not only one of the most loving things you can do for yourself, it's one of the most loving things you can do for others. Allowing others to say and do things that negatively impact people they are in relationship with is not loving. Colluding in other people's choices to not do their own work to show up better in relationships is not loving. Teaching our kids they can say and do whatever they want, whenever they want, is not loving, and isn't a life skill serving them in their future. Setting boundaries is an example of self-love and protects your well-being.

What Boundary Type/s Are You?

Most people have a mix of boundary types, and boundaries vary from relationship to relationship and within different contexts. I might have healthy boundaries around my work, yet fall back at family dinners into behavior patterns where I'm either too rigid or too porous. The flip side could also be true. Simplistically speaking, there are three types of boundaries, detailed in the next few paragraphs.

Rigid boundaries make us closed off to others and unable to make real connections. This type of boundary is a type of self-protection, or armor, and can lead to aloofness and detachment. Individuals with rigid boundaries tend to avoid intimacy, they don't ask for help and have very few close relationships, if any. And watch out if you make a relational mistake! There can be little room for grace, accountability and repairs with someone who has rigid boundaries. If you are in relationship with a person who has rigid boundaries, whether it's a coworker, partner or family member, you might experience some (or a lot) of negative energy if you make a mistake, or are perceived to have made a mistake. Much of cancel culture is an example of having rigid boundaries. In many cases there seems to be no room to experience the humanity and/or witnessing the path toward repair of the person who was canceled. If someone doesn't choose a path toward repair, by all means set a boundary. At this point a boundary would be considered healthy, not rigid.

Porous boundaries are the opposite of rigid boundaries. Someone with porous boundaries tends to overshare personal information, has difficulty saying no and gets over-involved in the lives of others. People with porous boundaries generally rely on others in order to feel good, or them feeling good depends on the opinions of others. These are the people-pleasers and provers. People with porous boundaries can be energy vampires, sucking the life out of others because they take up so much physical and mental space. I call it "bleeding all over people." When we don't have a strong sense of self, with healthy boundaries, our stuff pours out all over the place. For the person with porous boundaries AND for people they are in relationship with, life can often be exhausting.

Individuals with **healthy** boundaries value their own opinions over others. They don't compromise their values for others and they share personal information in appropriate ways. They know their own needs and wants and communicate them kindly and firmly to others. People with healthy boundaries are also accepting when others set boundaries because they are familiar with what setting healthy boundaries looks like. People with healthy boundaries experience more positive feelings in general, because they are adept at protecting their energy and have more good thoughts and feelings about themselves and others. Boundaried individuals take responsibility for themselves and their experiences.

Let's break down healthy boundary setting so you can pick a place to start your practice. Even if you believe you are skilled at setting boundaries, there's always room for growth. Always. And remember, if someone doesn't respond well to boundaries, it's most likely because they struggle to have or set healthy boundaries themselves. You can't make someone have healthy boundaries, you can only model to others what having boundaries and sticking by them looks like. Here's another reminder to care, but not carry. Rinse and repeat. Again, you might think setting boundaries doesn't feel loving or kind, but it can be one of the most loving, courageous and kind things you do for yourself AND for others.

Love Note: Our feelings are what signal to us a boundary needs to be set, or if a boundary has been crossed. In my experience, the feelings most associated with a lack of healthy boundaries or boundaries being crossed are anxiety, resentment, anger and disgust. We feel feelings in our bodies, so it's really important to have the skill of dropping out of our heads and into our bodies in order to tap into the wisdom our bodies hold. Our bodies have a way of knowing, yet this knowing can be clouded with so much unhelpful wiring we can't feel what we need to feel, or if we do feel something, we talk ourselves out of boundaries. Thankfully, this is something that can be healed and grown.

One of the first things you must do in order to establish healthy boundaries is to **get to know yourself**. Boundary setting is about YOU and what you can control (only your own thoughts, feelings and behaviors). Boundary setting is about what you will think, say and do in situations we can anticipate (your family always pressures you into drinking over holidays and you don't want to drink this year) and can't anticipate (your new boss wants you available to check-in via email on your vacation). It is our individual responsibility to teach people how to treat us, but we can't set healthy boundaries if we don't know how we feel about what's okay or not okay. To know ourselves, we might need to drown out voices from well-meaning people, and trust our brains and bodies to let us know when a boundary needs to be set. We need to be open to establishing new wiring. Have you done a value exercise recently (see the Dive Deeper Resources)? If not, I highly recommend you complete one online so you're grounded in what matters to you. Knowing what you hold in high regard is helpful when setting healthy boundaries. Being able to identify and be comfortable with your emotions, beliefs and ideas makes decisions about boundaries easier to make! For example, if one of my values is family but long periods of time around family are challenging, setting a healthy boundary could look like making my usual week-long visit a two-day visit instead because this is what feels best for my nervous systems. Setting healthy boundaries aligning with my value of family could also look like me leaving work on time so I can be present for my pets and partner when I get home.

When someone makes a request, or something comes up where we need to make a decision, pause and check in with yourself. This is easier said than done for many reasons. Trauma, for example, can make this practice difficult. So can anxiety, or other uncomfortable feelings and unhelpful stories wired into our brains, so if this is you, go slowly. Build up tolerance over time to be IN YOUR BODY so you can discover what boundary needs setting. Seeking professional help so you feel supported in this experience might be a good idea. Years and years of unhealthy boundaries, and acting outside of what's best for our bodies, can make the work to unravel things challenging, but inviting a pause will help tremendously. We often move through life on autopilot, constantly reacting to stimuli. This is a learned behavior, so it can be unlearned by training your brain and body to pause, check in and buy yourself some time to make decisions from a thoughtful place. Thought triangles are the perfect tool to guide you towards a pause. Below is an example of an unhelpful thought followed by a reworked triangle.

Initial Thought: They will think I'm a bitch if I tell them I can't make it to the party. I can't stand it when someone is upset with me!

Feelings: Fear, sadness, guilt, anxiety

Behavior: I go to the event anyways even though I was burned/maxed out, or I make up a lie about why I can't make the party, I grovel to my friend, I over-apologize

Reworked Thought: I hate to cancel on my friend and I do need a breather. My body is telling me I need a night in with no drinking or socializing, and a snuggle with my pet sounds nice. It's just a regular get-together so I feel okay about canceling. My friend might be disappointed and that's okay. It's important for me to take care of me.

Feelings: Still some fear, sadness, guilt and anxiety but A LOT less so. I feel more calm and relieved because I've been practicing listening to my body and I'm doing it!

Behavior: I let the party host know I can't make it but that I really appreciate the invite! I tell them I hope I can make it next time. I get into my favorite jammies, curl up on the couch with some tea and make a note in my phone to tell my therapist at our next session about my boundary setting victory!

As you get to know yourself, you might make mistakes in boundary setting. No worries! We're human and making mistakes is part of the process. When we make mistakes, we can have do-overs and make repairs (read more about these in Chapter Nine). We might also swing from being too rigid in our boundary setting to too porous, in other words, you might communicate in an unkind way, or say yes when you really need to say no. You might have said yes to helping out with a school function because of mom guilt, but with a major work deadline looming, you're constantly exhausted. At first, doing work on ourselves can be effortful because we are restructuring neural pathways, which requires a lot of energy from our brain. When you overcommit, sometimes you can back out and other times you need to follow through. Other people don't necessarily need to carry an extra load because you made a boundary mistake. If you can't back out or have some regret after backing out, run a future scenario in your mind where an opportunity is presented to you, and practice allowing yourself a moment to pause and check in with yourself. Learn to not make decisions on the spot!

A tip to help you invite the pause. Have a memorized phrase you say to people when they ask you to do something, or when you feel put on the spot. Something like "Let me check my schedule and I'll call or email you back with an answer." A phrase like this allows you to pause, reflect and check in with yourself about how the request makes you feel. This is a helpful process when setting boundaries in relationships too. Pause and check in with yourself when the person you are in relationship with says or does something that brings up uncomfortable feelings. Try not to react! Use your Feel Good Plan to first soothe your nervous systems, then consider whether a boundary needs to be set. "I really wish you hadn't said that. Next time, please be more thoughtful with your words" or, if you need to, let the issue go. A pause is helpful for situations when we need to set boundaries we didn't anticipate.

For situations we might encounter regularly or often, I encourage you to spend time in self-reflection to determine if you need boundaries. For example, ask yourself, "What will I think, say and/or do when … (insert any scenario here, like when your mom comments on your body, your dad makes his horrible joke at the dinner table or your friend cancels on you because better plans came along). Be careful you are not thinking about what you want them NOT to do, but are thinking about what YOU will think, say and/or do.

The next step in setting healthy boundaries is to not expect the other person to read your mind, but to **clearly and kindly communicate boundaries** to them. Don't leave anything up to chance. An uncommunicated boundary isn't in your best interest or the highest good of others. If boundaries go uncommunicated, resentment can build and disconnection can be created. Even within long standing relationships, clear communication of boundaries is necessary. No matter how long we've known someone, we can't expect them to read our minds.

When communicating boundaries, how much and how often we communicate depends on a few factors. Sometimes it's important to explain why you are setting a boundary, and other times you don't need to give any explanation or details at all. And those are just the two ends of the spectrum. There are lots of possibilities in between a full explanation and no explanation. Explaining the whys behind parenting decisions, for example, can teach children valuable life skills like critical thinking and personal responsibility. If a boundary needs to be communicated, but you find you can't thoughtfully explain the boundary, you may be operating from the automatic, fear-based, or less self-aware parts of your brain. Remember, we want to be regulated when setting boundaries, with the obvious exception being around personal safety. Another time it might be helpful to explain the whys behind a boundary is with romantic partners. Doing this creates connection and understanding, and can shift thought and behavior patterns towards becoming more helpful. Be patient with the process of stepping into vulnerability. You will almost certainly fuck up a few interactions, but you will be okay if you do. It can be both! Remember, you are also practicing tools to help you recover from mistakes.

Be aware, the first time you communicate boundaries, the other person might be so caught off guard they roll with it. The second time, though, they will be ready. They might be thinking, "Oh no you didn't." Stand firm, don't second-guess yourself and use your Feel Good Plan to manage any discomfort that arises. This process gets easier! Although setting boundaries can be messy at times, as you practice and become more skilled, you will also give others permission to do the same. Relationships get infinitely better when two boundaried people show up in them. I have a friend who says, "Your yeses, nos and not right nows are welcome here" when she makes a request. What a nice way to invite others to set a boundary if they need to.

To find your own boundary setting boundary if they need to. To find your own boundary setting phrases, try some of these boundary setting sentence stems to see how they land for you.

- I'd like you to listen and not problem solve right now (or vice versa).
- I need a few moments to myself. Can we finish this conversation in a bit when I'm ready?
- Let me check my calendar and I'll get back to you. Can I email or text you my response?
- I can't promise anything right now. Let me take stock of what I have going on and then check in with myself to see if I have capacity for another responsibility.
- Thank you for thinking of me! I'd really like the opportunity but I need to check in with my partner about the impact it

- would have on our family. Let me get back to you. Is there a timeline for when you need to hear back from me?

Practice communicating boundaries from a place of emotional regulation, otherwise a boundary can land as a demand, or a reaction from our parts, rather than from our adult self with prefrontal cortexes online. Soothe those nervous systems with Feel Good Plans before using kind and firm (both are important) words to communicate what is okay and not okay for you. If we are only kind, we can come across as passive and people-pleasing. If we are only firm, we can come across as rigid and rude. An important note, this is not an invitation to tone police people in your life. We all have different ways of communicating as a result of individual races and cultures, for example, and while we can always take feedback as humans in relationship with other humans, it is not okay to dismiss what someone is communicating to you because you don't like their tone. Tone policing is a commonly used defense mechanism distracting from the actual content someone is communicating. If you're unfamiliar with this phrase, I encourage you to google it and find more resources to support your understanding.

Next in setting healthy boundaries is to **prepare for fallout**. Sounds ominous, and it can be at first. When you practice boundary setting, especially with people you have established unhealthy behavior patterns with, be ready for some pushback. If you've always been a YES person, the first time you say NO might be a little dicey for everyone. If you've played the role of caregiver to everyone but yourself, but now want to create space for yourself, it might be uncomfortable for everyone. This is the challenging part of setting boundaries, where you need to let go of the need to be liked or the fear of hurting or disappointing others and reconnect to your values and what your body is communicating to you. Unfortunately, you might need to distance yourself, over the short- or long-term, from people who don't respect boundaries. This could be physical, as in actual distance, or it could be psychological distance, meaning you don't allow certain people to take up as much of your mental space.

Healthy boundary setting within intimate relationships, such as with romantic partners or family members, can be especially tricky because you are changing long standing behavior patterns. Adapting to the preferences of others, or having rigid or porous boundaries, might have been a coping strategy you used to create emotional or physical safety as a child or teen. Boundary setting is an area where old stories can definitely come up, so do the best you can to notice uncomfortable feelings, soothe your nervous systems with Feel Good Plans and maybe ask yourself some helpful questions. What's the worst thing that can happen if I set a boundary here? What is the best thing that can happen if I set a boundary here? What do I think might actually happen? This exercise helps your brain become familiar with different scenarios and helps it stay out of fear mode as much as possible.

Detaching from the responses and reactions of others as they are impacted by boundaries is an important part of this work. I often hear clients tell me they don't want to bother with setting a boundary because they don't believe it will be honored. I remind them this part of setting boundaries doesn't matter as much as they might think it does. It would be lovely, dreamy even, if we set healthy boundaries and everyone honored them. The reality is, when others show up in ways we want/need when boundaries are set it's a BONUS, not a must or a given. You may wonder what the point of setting boundaries is then! One benefit is you feel empowered to speak your truth and then behave in ways honoring yourself. There is a lot of healing and growing occurring just from changing our own behaviors and creating safer spaces for yourself and your parts. We also increase self-trust, which means we believe there is nothing we can't navigate, we stay true to ourselves, we look after our own needs and safety and we treat ourselves with love and compassion instead of striving for perfection. Another major benefit is data collection! When we communicate a boundary and it isn't honored, this is information for you to sift through to determine your future behavior and level of connection with the other person.

When it comes to boundaries, it is VERY important to repeat over and over again, you can care but not carry. You can care about the other person, that your boundary may not be what they want, but you don't need to carry their reaction to your boundary. This is too heavy a burden and not yours to carry. Their job is to take care of themselves no matter what they experience, just as it is YOUR job to take care of you and your feelings. Many might experience uncomfortable consequences as a result of setting boundaries, such as the shifting or ending of relationships. The other person might choose to move on.

We can control how much personal access we give others. How many portals into our lives we open up. This is a difficult concept for most brains to grasp, because there are parts of us wanting everyone to like and accept us. We want to be good and kind. We want others to feel good! Consider we might also have parts of ourselves stuck at younger ages, putting a lot of significance on mattering and belonging to other people, especially our childhood caregivers, even though they were or are hurtful or harmful. As children, the significance was necessary because we relied on them for OUR VERY SURVIVAL. Our younger parts might still try to lead us to believe you will not be okay if those relationships aren't the same. First and foremost, we need to soothe our younger parts with things like a Feel Good Plan and by practicing a master's level of healthy emotional processing. From there, get curious about why your younger parts are triggered. What needs to heal and grow so those parts don't show up as much in ways out of alignment with your adult skill set and values?

I believe it's truly in the highest good of everyone involved for you to honor boundaries you feel you need to set. When we don't set healthy boundaries, we continue to collude or facilitate the very behaviors we wish we didn't have to navigate. Read this again. We play a role in the negative behavior patterns of others when we don't develop skills to set healthy boundaries.

If you're feeling indulgent, try the following practice to help you shift towards healthier boundaries and experience more joy and connection with yourself.

- **Sit comfortably** in a chair or on your bed. Close your eyes if comfortable for your nervous systems. If it isn't, soften your gaze on the wall or another object to reduce visual noise.

- **Take a few deep breaths** and connect to your body through your breaths. Maybe place a hand on your belly or chest to be more intentional with the connection.

- Now **imagine your future self in your mind's eye,** the you existing a year from now. Imagine your future self standing in front of you. What is their posture like? What expression do they have on their face? Picture them standing close enough to you that they are clasping your hands. Take in every detail you can. Optionally, picture your future self filled with or surrounded by a certain color of energy. What color is it? How bright is it? Is it sparkly or opaque? Then imagine your current self breathing in the energy until it fills every part of your body and begins to seep out your pores.

- Next, **ask your future self** what is the next best step to take to have healthier boundaries. How do you get from where you are now in your boundary practice, to where they are a year from now?

- **Listen for an answer,** thank them and let them know you'll connect back with them again soon.

- **Come back from your inner world** to your present space by   noticing something you hear, feel or see. Notice how you feel in your body (hopefully something like a sense of calm and resolve) and write down your takeaways from the experience.

Practice Self-Compassion

Changing brain wiring through healthy boundary setting, or any other helpful shift in skill set, requires a lot of self-compassion to minimize self-sabotage as much as possible. When you are giving your brain new instructions like, "I don't need to say and do everything perfectly, I can make mistakes and be okay" or "I can pause and be more mindful when I feel uncomfortable," it might take some time for your brain to get on board because your brain wants to be "right." If you've been telling yourself for years things like, "I have to be perfect," "I'm a failure" or "I have to do everything myself," your brain is going to find evidence to reinforce those narratives before adopting new instructions.

Consider the scenario of a toddler learning to walk. The toddler is creating new neural pathways as they practice this new skill, and learning to walk takes some time. At first, each step is wobbly, and the toddler falls often. As motor mapping solidifies, though, the kiddo falls less and less. When babies fall down, we don't shame them or scold them or tell them they never should have tried walking in the first place. Why then do we say and think these things as adults? We are creating new neural pathways and rewiring our brain, and we too deserve the same, "Oh that looks like it hurts, let's keep trying" said with the same compassionate voice we give little ones.

When we challenge old narratives and change wiring, we can at times fall back into old patterns of behavior and narratives, primarily around where we haven't been successful. Our inner critic can be so loud, right? This is our moment of choice. First, create awareness that what you are experiencing might be old wiring. Next, give your brain a pep talk with your new narrative. Say something like, "Oh that's my old story, my new story is I really enjoy taking care of myself and I'm proud of even the smallest changes I'm making each day." Finally, notice what you are doing differently and better than before. What small changes in your brain wiring are already evident?

Love Note: My friends, so many of us have really unhelpful brain connections around the term self-compassion. We have parts of ourselves equating self-kindness with laziness ("I won't get anything done if I talk to myself nicely."), which is a sign of internalized oppression, among other things. If your brain or your parts show up negatively with the words self-care or self-compassion, then choose different words that work for you. Also, you can tell your brain, "Hey, we're doing things differently now. We are going to love ourselves into doing things, instead of doing things the old way." When we love ourselves forward we have more energy to actually do what we need to do. Give it a go!

Self-sabotage is simply the brain trying to be right, and trying to find evidence for old narratives to be true. So, change the narrative and you'll decrease the likelihood of making choices contradicting your goals. When you do fall down, which you will because you're creating new neural pathways, offer yourself compassion. Nurture yourself by saying something like, "It's okay brain, we had a little dip there but let's get back on track because remember, our goal is to be able to have energy to keep up with the kids." In the beginning, rewiring and coming up with replacement narratives is a lot of effort, but the more often you remind your brain of the new narrative, the more the new narrative will become your default. Your brain will become more effective in looking for evidence you DO want to be more active, or more calm in the mornings with the kids, and before you know it your new narrative will become more and more true and you will have made it to the "make it" part of "fake it until you make it."

So, what are your new narratives? What do you envision for yourself? You really do get to decide what they will be! Do you want to be a more calm, mindful parent and/or partner? Be a kinder, gentler person even when you're feeling overwhelmed? Do you want to take feedback at work in a more positive way? Maybe work towards the career you've had in the back of your mind for years? Do you want to take care of your brain and body in better ways? Maybe your boundaries are too rigid, or too porous, and you want to make healthier connections with others? Think back to the reason you bought this book, what did you imagine for yourself when you did? Get as detailed as possible and repeat the new narratives often. Also, what compassionate message can you give yourself when you have a little dip (hint: use a thought triangle to do this).

Often, we take better care of others than we do ourselves. We cannot give what we don't have, though, so that compassion you're showing others but not yourself? It could be coming from a place of shoulding (I should do this or that), a place of propping up your sense of self or a place of feeling at your best when serving others, but you're having a hard time giving yourself the same. It could be a trauma response. It could be coming from a genuine place of care, but if you're not giving it to yourself too, it's not coming from a WHOLE place.

These days we hear a lot about the importance of self-care (aka acts of self-compassion). You might be familiar with the oxygen mask analogy, and while it seems cliche and overused, it's actually the perfect analogy for self-compassion. If you've flown on an airplane, you know flight attendants ask that in the case of an emergency, you put an oxygen mask on yourself first, and then put one on your kid or another vulnerable person. We can't love people in our lives in the best ways possible if they get all the oxygen and we end up passed out or burned out.

Particularly if we have kids, it's important for us to model how wonderful adulthood can be so they want to experience it too! Many of us make adulthood look very uninteresting to say the least. Another way to visualize self-compassion I like even more is the teacup and saucer analogy. When we give ourselves love and compassion, we fill up our cup and allow the overflow to spill onto the saucer. When we love and care for others, we should use the overflow of love and care on the saucer, not the love and care from our own cup. The cup is for us! This way, our own cup stays full yet we have a constant overflow of love and compassion to give others.

You've already been practicing some of the best strategies for developing self-compassion. You're using a Feel Good Plan (essentially a list of things you can think, say and do to offer yourself compassion), you're developing awareness around what your thought triangles are and you're reworking them to be more helpful for you. Healthy boundary setting is one of the most compassionate things you can do for yourself, and you're working on setting those. I hope that as you're practicing these strategies, you're noticing you are thinking, feeling, saying and doing better towards yourself. You're noticing how much more self-compassion you give yourself. If you haven't noticed these things yet, take a minute to reflect. Have you been kinder to yourself? In what ways?

Love Note: When you practice self-compassion you are showing the world what loving you looks like. You're showing your younger parts, who could have needed compassion desperately, how to be loved. You're showing others how to love you by how you love yourself. And most importantly, if you're a parent and you would like to instill the value of compassion in your kids, they aren't only looking at how you love them, they are also watching how you love yourself.

Self-Reflection

- What have you been modeled and taught about boundaries? Compare how you were modeled and taught to what you've learned about boundaries in this book and other places.
- Do you have any models of healthy boundary setting? Even on social media or in the shows you watch?
- What are some boundary setting shifts you want to make? Identify a boundary, even a teeny tiny one, you could set in your personal life. How about your professional life?
- What are ways you give yourself compassion? What can you add to the list?
- What song lyrics from *this is how I learn to say no* by EMELINE do you think fit this chapter and why? Message me on social media and I'll select my three favorite responses to win a signed copy of the book!

Affirmations

- Setting healthy boundaries is tricky for me right now and it will get easier with time. I can't wait to see what a boundary setting expert I become!
- It's okay to say no.
- My time and energy are valuable. I am careful how I spend it!
- I can care about others without carrying stuff that is theirs to carry. I am responsible for my own thoughts, feelings and behaviors and they are responsible for theirs.
- I choose to love myself. I show myself care and compassion everyday.

Dive Deeper Resources

Section
Two

Relational Discovery (You/We)

CHAPTER 7

Putting Your Learning to Work

Listen to Crowded Table *by The Highwomen,*
I Ain't Mad At Cha *by 2Pac*
and I Can Change *by Lake Street Dive*

You made it through Section One, the self-discovery section! You're now more aware of what your inner landscape is, where you might want to heal and grow and have more awareness of what you bring to relationships. You also have a better understanding of what your relationship partners bring to the table, because every human has a complex and beautiful inner landscape too! Everything you've read so far is foundational to healthy relationships, so let's get into how to put some relational theories and strategies into practice.

A Relational Framework

Hopefully by now you see each of us having our own inner world from which we bring parts to our relationships. As we move into developing more relational skills, a framework to keep in mind is each of us brings our own world into relational spaces. At times, in relationships, we need to move out of our own world and into the world of the other person, especially when the other person is experiencing emotional distress of any kind. When our partners are expressing uncomfortable emotions, EVEN IF WE'RE THE ONES WHO TRIGGERED THEM, we want to try to move into the other person's world and be with them there, without trying to get them out of their world and into ours. Confused? Let me show you what I mean.

Personal Scenario: Couples counseling with our amazing therapist. I bring up an interaction between my husband and me I'd like to dig into, and lo and behold, when we do, I find underneath my behavior is a childhood wound. I'm triggered and crying as I share the connection I've made to some early childhood trauma. In the moment, I am in my own world, vulnerably expressing hurt having nothing to do with my husband, but hurt that was triggered by the interaction we had before therapy.

Husband's Reaction: My husband is shocked at what I'm sharing and begins to ask questions about the details of what I'm sharing as a way to (subconsciously) bring me into his world, which is decidedly less painful. He wants to know the whats, whys and hows of the trauma. He's trying to ease my pain, but in ways I experience as shutting down the topic. He's "fixing," and not holding space for me. I feel confused, disoriented and frustrated with his reaction along with all of the other feelings I was experiencing prior to his response.

Therapist's Reaction: Our therapist invites my husband to pause and watch how she models entering my world. Our therapist turns to me and reflects back what she heard me say. She nods and makes affirming statements like, "I get that" and "Okay, I see." She asks me questions like, "Is there anything else?" and "What was that like for you?" As she enters my world, instead of trying to bring me into hers, my nervous systems calm down. I feel seen and heard and am able to be less engulfed in the triggered emotions. My husband then makes the necessary shifts and the rest of the session is very productive.

We often unknowingly try to ease someone else's distress by bringing them into our own world instead of being with them in theirs. This can be, in certain contexts, a form of gaslighting. Anytime we want someone else to live in OUR reality ("It's not that bad, you're overreacting" or "Why does this bother you so much? If it were me, I wouldn't care so much about it"), even if we are trying to benefit them, we can be gaslighting.

Check Your Weapons and Armor At the Door

Because of our wiring (those sometimes pesky thought and behavior patterns), each of us more than likely has weapons and armor we put on when we feel uncomfortable. Weapons can be anything from the words we use and how we use them, to how we posture and use our bodies, to actual weapons. Armor can be diversion tactics like tone policing, getting stuck in the details of an incident ("I didn't actually say it that way" or "I gave you the look after dinner, not before"), semantics, stonewalling, the silent treatment and so much more. What are your weapons of war and ways you defend against (armor against) feedback, accountability and/or discomfort in general? If you're stuck, ask your partner or a close friend. I'm sure they will have ideas for you!

Love Note: Parts of ourselves can be very protective of our vulnerabilities and we can appreciate them for it! How clever and helpful of them! When we become aware of thoughts and behaviors we want to shift, all we need to do is to have compassion for ourselves. We can say things like, "Hey brain, we don't need to use these strategies anymore. We are safe and can figure this out. Thank you for trying to help but we are going to try something different this time. We are going to practice taking deep breaths and staying calm while we give/receive feedback (or whatever is happening at the moment)."

Support Healthy Relationship Dynamics: Schedule It

If your goal is to show up differently and better in relationships so you can experience more joy and connection, then as much as you have the skill and capacity in the moment, check your weapons and armor at the door. This might seem difficult if you have behavior patterns with your partner to discuss feedback and conflict IN THE MOMENTS following the incident, or before either or both of you have calmed your nervous systems. I have a simple strategy you can practice to help move you away from this pattern and increase your ability to be present and open when discussing something difficult. Maybe you have tension and conflict around different parenting styles, the division of household labor, sex, finances, not using a turn signal when driving or constant lateness, WHATEVER it is for you and your partner, this one tool can be a gamechanger if consistently practiced. The tool I'm talking about is scheduling weekly check-ins. Friendships require less frequent check-ins, and co-workers even less often, but do consider other types of relationships might also benefit from this tool. If you're a parent, definitely schedule weekly check-ins with your kids if they are age four or older.

So, you're asking me to schedule the communication of my frustration? Yes, yes I am. In order for our nervous systems to be in an open and receiving place, a place fostering the most possible connection, we need to experience safety and predictability. Setting time aside each week, preferably around the same time and day, allows you to move through your days and weeks with more calm and stability. What we typically do instead is pepper each other's nervous systems with stuff as it arises, which often means our weapons and armor come out after too many hits.

My partner and I picked Sunday afternoons and have titled the calendar entry "THE MOST FUN TIME EVER." Naming the entry came about after we discovered one of us (not me, ha) had blocks to check-ins, so calling it something silly and sarcastic helped overcome the block. Do what you need to do to make it happen! Check-ins should be protected as much as possible, so make a commitment to give this tool at least six or eight weeks before you throw in the towel. Give it a real go! You can use the time not just to share things pissing you off, it can also be a time to celebrate individual wins and wins as a couple, calendar for the week/month, set intentions, get to know each other better, make a meal or have a snuggle.

We always begin with victories, especially if we've been working on developing certain skills or practices individually or as a couple. Paying attention to victories gives instructions to our brains we want more of them! Sharing wins first is also energizing to our work because we notice healing and growing as it's happening. Celebrating victories also speeds us along our self-discovery and relational paths. After victories, we move into reviewing the upcoming calendar before moving to giving and receiving feedback. We usually end with some questions to help us connect and/or set intentions for the week. This is also a good time to go over needs or wants for whatever you're navigating as an individual or as a couple.

This doesn't sound so bad, right! It may seem simple and silly, but imagine a week where you aren't being nagged or picked at, or only interacting in ways disconnecting and negative. Sounds dreamy right? This does take some practice, as we often move through our days and weeks on autopilot, or in reactionary ways. I highly recommend keeping a note in your phone where you keep track of issues coming up or vent your frustrations through writing. Jot down details about interactions and how you feel or felt. What you might find is when you look at your notes before check-ins, it's still a thing, it's less of a thing or it's no longer a thing. What you are essentially doing is inviting a nice, long pause into relational spaces to give your nervous systems a break, process interactions and thoughtfully determine how you want to navigate going forward.

Part of your process between interactions you choose to write down for check-ins, and the actual check-in, might be to chat about the interaction with a trusted friend. I'm all for asking friends to listen and/or offer me advice and perspective. Just be cautious to avoid who I call "flame fanners." You know who they are! They are the people you bring your issue to, and by the time you leave the conversation, the issue is bigger and you feel worse because they added fuel to the fire.

Instead, share with people who are willing to hold you accountable, help you see where areas of growth are and with whom you feel seen and heard. Another part of processing what you want to bring to a check-in can be to ask yourself some reflective questions like, "How did I feel during and after the interaction?" "What is mine to own in the interaction and what is not mine to own?" "What is my truth and how will I communicate it?" or "Does how I showed up connect to any patterns I'm trying to disrupt or wounds I'm trying to heal?"

Support Healthy Relationship Dynamics: Set the Picnic

What if you think scheduling a check-in sounds like the worst idea you've ever heard, or you have an urgent concern that can't wait? Well, you can set a picnic. Our couple's counselor uses this metaphor for making room in your mental spaces and schedules to discuss difficult topics and give each other feedback outside of formal check-ins. Here are the basics. Say you're out for a walk with a friend and all of a sudden you say, "Hey, let's have a picnic! I brought a blanket and some crackers. What did you bring?" Your friend, however, had it in their mind you were just going for a walk, so they didn't bring any food AND just wanted to walk and talk. What a shitty picnic! Now, if you say to your friend beforehand, "How do you feel about having a little picnic at some point on our walk? I can bring fried chicken and drinks. What would you like to bring?" Your friend can then say yes or no to a picnic, and if they say yes, they can offer what they'd like to bring. No surprises, and most likely you're going to have a lovely time together.

We often surprise our partners, colleagues, kids and friends with feedback. We feel the need to talk about what's on our mind in the moment, or whenever WE want to talk about it. Setting up purposeful conversations instead, and making them aware beforehand the topic(s) you'd like to discuss, can better help them prepare. Here's an example of what I'm talking about.

Partner 1: Hey, I've got some things I need your help making sense of. I think thirty minutes would be enough time. Do you have capacity to talk?

Partner 2: I had a shit day at work. I was really looking forward to just watching a show together because I need some down time. I'm afraid I won't be able to show up how I want to in the conversation. Is it urgent?

Partner 1: It's not "tonight urgent," but I'd like to talk to you by tomorrow at the latest. Can you get yourself in the headspace to talk?

Partner 2: I'll manage my day as best I can tomorrow so we can talk right after dinner. Sound good?

If the matter is urgent, Partner 2 could say something like, "Okay, give me forty-five minutes to get into a better headspace, then I should be ready to talk. What do you need me to bring to the picnic?" If a strategy like this leads to increased anxiety, keep the invitation as low-key as possible and pick something on your Feel Good Plan to help lower the intensity of the anxiety. As already stated, I recommend weekly check-ins for partnered relationships and families, but some things can't or don't need to wait until the weekly check-in. This will be something you practice, to evaluate what can and can't wait. I highly suggest you be selective though! The old adage pick your battles is applicable here.

We can set picnics to discuss all sorts of topics, not just the difficult ones, with just about anyone we are in relationship with! Have an upcoming visit with a friend who recently posted something on social media that surprised you? Do you wonder how your romantic partner or friend wants to be loved and appreciated by you (aka what is their love language)? In relationship with people who have very different opinions and experiences on topics like taxes, body autonomy, civil rights and safety for the LBGTQIA2S+ community, gender roles, religion, fair pay, educational access, Black Lives Matter or any other topic that often sends people to opposite corners of the boxing ring (or to the middle of the ring to duke it out)? If we want to experience more joy and connection in relationships, we need to practice having hard conversations. Setting a picnic, and the other tools and strategies I share in this book, allows us to show up ready to lean into topics producing a lot of discomfort, and therefore growth.

Love Note: Remember, as we disrupt outdated thought and behavior patterns, we need HELP. Help to create new neural pathways can come in the form of structures like scripts, steps to follow, sentence stems, weekly check-ins, taking time to rework thought triangles and so much more. This is why I'm summarizing and sharing my favorite structures here, and inviting you to dive deeper if you'd like!

Support Healthy Relationship Dynamics: Imago Dialogue

In more formal check-ins or in casual picnics, we still need help with what to say and how to say it. Otherwise, we might derail conversations and create less joy and less connection. Or no joy and no connection. To avoid these outcomes, I suggest practicing Imago Dialogue. Imago Relationship Therapy was developed decades ago by Helen LaKelly Hunt and Harville Hendrix as a way to relieve blame and shame and invite healing and growing in romantic partnerships. I was introduced to the modality when I read their book Getting the Love You Want, which you can find linked in the Dive Deeper Resources at the end of this chapter. Following the scripts and steps in their Imago Dialogue could be just the disruptor your wiring needs in order to develop more helpful ways of navigating conflict. Practicing their ways of sending and receiving in check-ins and picnics, when discussing topics you know are fraught with tension or may be activating to your partner, to you or to both, can be an anchor to nervous systems and provide some safety as you navigate difficult life stuff. If you need more support, search Imago Couples Therapists Near Me online and you should find several options.

In Imago Dialogue, there is a sender and a receiver. The sender is the person giving feedback, or practicing vulnerability in any way. The receiver is the person receiving the feedback, in other words the person who is actively listening by entering the world of the sender. Here is what an Imago Dialogue interaction might look like. If needed, switch roles after completing the interaction.

SENDER (says one or more of the following sentence stems)
I would like to dialogue about ... is now okay?
I feel ... I love ... I need ...
What's bothering me is ...

RECEIVER (practices the three steps in Imago Dialogue)

Step 1: Mirroring

Let me see if I've got you ... (reflects back what the sender sent, not necessarily verbatim)
I heard you say ... or ...
You said ... am I getting you? ... Did I get that?
Is there more about that?
Let me see if I got it all ...
Am I getting you?
Did I get all of that? or Is that a good summary?

Step 2: Validation

You make sense to me, and what makes sense is ...
I can understand that ... given that ...
I can see how you would see it that way because sometimes I do ...

Step 3: Empathy

I imagine you might be feeling ...
Is that what you're feeling?

The third step in Imago Dialogue invites empathy (I prefer to use the term compassion instead, I believe the research is more sound), and is when you get to enter the world of your partner and not make it (the conversation, issue, whatever the "it" is) about you and your world. This is where your Feel Good Plan, specifically helpful self-talk and deep breaths, come in handy. I've sat through numerous Imago Dialogues with my partner, and in our practice things have sometimes gone sideways because either or both of us get activated, or go off script and start infusing the discussion with our own thoughts, experiences and interpretations. STAY ON SCRIPT. Pretend you've memorized lines for a very important performance, and continue moving through the discomfort of trying something new. Remember, a huge part of any rewiring process is the "fake it until you make it" stage. New thought or behavior patterns might feel fake, awkward or untrue because you haven't thought it, said it or done it enough times for it to feel a part of your current reality and chosen brain wiring. All of this becomes more natural with practice. I promise. Until then, embrace the awkward!

Generalizing tools such as Imago Dialogue, check-ins or setting picnics, as well as self-discovery reminders I'll share in the next section are important to other parts of our lives, not just our romantic partnerships. Ask yourself, "How can I use these tools in my work environment to create safer, more predictable and increasingly positive spaces for people I work and lead with? How can I practice these tools with my kids, friends and family members?"

Love Note: Using structures like Imago Dialogue is something you can practice alone to increase active listening and communication skills and to shift relational dynamics. I also encourage you to let those you use this structure with know what you are doing. You might say something like, "I want to work on how I communicate and listen, especially when we have a conflict, so I'm going to be trying something new. I just wanted to let you know, because it will be different than how I typically show up. If you're curious, I can tell you more about what I'm doing." My dear readers, just say the thing! Let people know you're shaking things up!

Self-Discovery Reminders

Relationships can feel easier when we are mostly, or only, in community with people who look like, sound like and behave like us. AND being in community with people who don't look like, sound like or behave like us is how we create more joy and connection for ourselves locally and globally. Here are a few strategies to help you increase social awareness by putting all of this self-awareness into practice.

Reminder: Get Grounded in Your Locus of Control

Creating calm in our internal worlds, by trying to manage things out of our control, is a surefire way to experience relational disconnection, burnout, resentment, mental illness and more. Instead, move away from relying on external things, like other people's behaviors, to feel good more often. Work on developing a strong internal locus of control, which means we focus on what is within our control, essentially only our own thoughts, feelings and behaviors. Conflict will more often arise when we overextend ourselves into someone else's locus of control, and this can be exhausting too! Instead of developing a strong internal locus of control, we might be reinforcing an external locus of control, where we blame or rely on other people and things for our well-being. An example of external locus of control is the if/then, when/then model of happiness, which means we look outside ourselves to experience wellness. If our kids get good grades, or behave at the dinner party, then we are okay internally. If my boss is nice to me today, I'll have a good day or be okay internally. When I get a promotion, then I'll be set and happy. When I retire, then I'll have more time for my favorite hobby. If this year wasn't so difficult, then I would be able to take care of myself.

Here is a short activity to help you visualize and develop a stronger internal locus of control. You'll need some paper and a pen. First, draw a circle in the center of your paper. Inside the circle, identify everything you have control over. Outside the circle identify everything you don't have control over. Be as detailed as possible! What do you notice? If we pay attention to what we don't have control of, how do we feel most often? If we pay attention to what we do have control of, how do we feel more often and what kinds of decisions would we make from being in this place more often?

Reminder: Develop Perspective Taking

When we develop a strong internal locus of control, we increase our ability to take the perspectives of others. Perspective-taking is examining another person's point of view through the lens of our internal values and intentions. Let's do a quick run through of some strategies to develop perspective-taking so we can show up better in any relationship, but especially our intimate relationships.

Use self-regulation tools to get your nervous system in the space where it can consider others' experiences and have discussions without arguments. We can disagree without being disagreeable. Often, the things we have trouble accepting in others, we actually have trouble accepting in ourselves, so use the discomfort as a mirror and self-reflect!

Listen to understand, not to reply. Allow for silence and don't make it all about you and how it affects you. Imago Dialogue helps here!

Take your time. Respond, don't react! Use Feel Good Plans and thought triangles to increase Self-Awareness. We want to say and do from our prefrontal cortex (thinking brain), not from our uncomfortable feelings.

Be kind. We never want to be rude or dismissive of someone else's thoughts and feelings. Jokes, or comments at someone else's expense, are never funny and simply perpetuate stereotypes, inconsideration and even trauma.

Be curious about others. ASK QUESTIONS instead of making assumptions or making the conversation about you. Celebrate the wins and accomplishments of others. Make other people feel important.

Learn about identities unfamiliar to you, even ones making you feel uncomfortable. You can still hold strong to values and beliefs while increasing social awareness. Read personal accounts and autobiographies. Take in media reflecting the general population. Support and center marginalized folks. Get to know humanity on a deeper level in a variety of ways, especially in person.

Understand the importance of impact versus intent. More on this in the next chapter.

Be generous with assumptions. Use thought triangles to create more helpful and connecting stories about others.

Perspective-taking is accepting of diversity and respectful of the identities and experiences of others. It says, "I may not agree with you AND I can still show you I care and see you." Increasing your capacity to take perspective will improve your well-being and relationships. I choose to believe we have more in common than we don't AND those commonalities are easier to find when all humans involved are actively developing social and emotional intelligence. Finding common ground, or taking the perspective of someone who has the social and emotional skills of a child, can be tricky. When this is the case, choose your boundaries!

Reminder: Increase Your Ability to Recognize Bias

Biases are an outcome of our wiring, just like beliefs, and they sometimes play out in relationships in really harmful ways. A bias is a disproportionate weight in favor of, or against, an idea or thing, usually in closed-minded, prejudicial or unfair ways. Biases can be innate or learned (nurture and nature). In science and engineering, a bias is a systematic error, but in all other contexts we might want to consider them to be relational errors.

Cognitive Biases are mental shortcuts, and with all the information we take in on a daily basis, it only makes sense our brains want to take shortcuts when it comes to moving through life. This can sometimes be helpful and sometimes not. It's not helpful when our biases harm others. Our brains instinctively want to keep us comfortable and right, even if it means going against logic. In other words, when faced with decisions, our brains will often encourage us to make them based on the amount of information we have. The more info (certainty) we currently have, the more likely we are to choose what the info supports, even if logically it's not the best decision. You can see how this could be an issue in relationships! We can uncover hidden biases in several ways, including the following:

- Acknowledge biases are a thing. Bring what is implicit (subconscious) to the explicit (consciousness).
- Allow yourself and others time to show you who they are. Sometimes this can take a while!
- Understand stereotypes and how they influence thought process, feelings and behaviors
- Be open to possibility
- Stretch comfort zones with novel experiences. Notice what comes up for you as you do!

There are tons of great resources online to help you uncover biases. I appreciate the Harvard Implicit Associations Test for creating awareness of neural connections. The test helps uncover wiring we probably didn't install ourselves, but wiring that might be reinforcing how we move through life. Learning for Justice has some great tools and content on their website too. Both of these resources can be found in the Dive Deeper section at the end of the chapter.

Increasing our self and social awareness helps us remove as many obstacles as possible to being in healthy relationship with other human beings. This means we put our best effort forward in order to create safer, kinder spaces for all. This chapter directly connects with the earlier chapter on beliefs, where I mentioned all beliefs are okay unless they are harmful to yourself and/or others. A lack of perspective taking, implicit and explicit biases and a desire to overextend ourselves into others' loci of control harms ourselves and others. When we don't allow others the dignity of healthy options, the ability to choose for themselves what they need for their own well-being, then we are harming others. We are also harming ourselves, because the impact of unwell people on our communities is felt by everyone. The need to control other people and their environments in order to experience safety and calm within ourselves is not authentic. Consider where you might be over or underextending yourself (not participating in community) and see if shifts could support your individual and relational well-being.

Self-Reflection

- What do you identify as your relational armor and weapons?
- What tool or strategy from this chapter do you want to practice and with whom?
- What other takeaways do you have from this chapter?
- What song lyrics from *Crowded Table* by The Highwomen, *I Ain't Mad At Cha* by 2Pac and *I Can Change* by Lake Street Dive do you think fit this chapter and why? Message me on social media and I'll select my three favorite responses to win a signed copy of the book!

Affirmations

- I am in charge of my own thoughts, feelings and behaviors. I'm sovereign over my own experience and other people are sovereign over theirs. I'm developing a strong internal locus of control.
- Let's shake it up, what affirmations would you choose for yourself from this chapter?

Dive Deeper Resources

CHAPTER 8

Make Conflict Your Bitch, Part One

Listen to Don't Wanna Fight *by Alabama Shakes
and* Blindsided *by Kelsea Ballerini*

For most, this is going to be a doozy of a chapter, but the good news is successfully navigating conflict in relationships is simply a skill set. Nothing mysterious about it. So what makes conflict so scary to most people? Navigating conflict is one of those relational experiences we all have stories about, and those stories often come with uncomfortable feelings. So much of how we manage relational discomfort connects to what was modeled to us by our primary caregivers. How did they handle conflict? Shout it out? Fight dirty, with name-calling and gaslighting? Stuff it down until everything blows up like Mount Saint Helens in 1980? Never saw your caregivers disagree about anything? What does your culture teach you about navigating conflict? We were modeled and taught a mixed bag of how to handle disagreement, and it's our responsibility as adults to sift through the wiring and decide what we want to keep and what we want to shift. Time to update the software!

A lot of conflict can be resolved when we develop the skills to give and receive feedback. That's it! We don't know what we don't know, so hearing from others things we can work on to be more relational is essential to healthy relationships. Where do you get your feedback from? Identify sources from which you get feedback, such as your boss, romantic partner, kids, friends or society in general. If you have few sources of feedback and/or you complain about people giving you feedback, then ask yourself questions like these.

- Do I gaslight, defend or shut down when someone cares enough to give me feedback, or am I a safe person for others to give feedback to?
- If I have defense mechanisms towards feedback, what can I shift in what I think, say and do to allow space for more people to come to me?
- What sources do I value feedback from the most?
- Who do I tend to dismiss when it comes to their feedback? Why?
- Which relationships do I care the most about?
- How can I be more open to feedback?
- Do I have people in my life who have the skills to give feedback in helpful ways?

Friends, learning to navigate conflict in healthy ways is some dark room shit. Let me explain what I mean by that. You know the feeling when you enter an unfamiliar, pitch black room? You're on high alert, stressed, anxious and the uncertainty of what lies ahead feels overwhelming. This is what individual and relational work can feel like, dark room shit. So next time you're experiencing uncomfortable feelings while thinking, saying or doing something new, remind yourself this is just dark room shit and know you can do it! You're developing skills to manage the experience and you're okay.

I've learned over the years to appreciate conflict because of its many benefits. Conflict allows us to deepen relationships in ways other relational strategies can't provide. Yes, I just identified conflict as a relational strategy! When we learn to handle relational difficulties with boundaries, and in regulated and compassionate ways, we experience infinite possibilities in how we can heal and grow as individuals and as a global community. When conflict arises, and either or both parties involved don't have the skill, will or capacity to navigate the situation, then yes, the relationship might take a turn for the worse or end. AND this is okay. You will be okay. Not every relationship can, will or should last. We may experience hurt, anger, sadness, pain and so much more, AND all of this is part of the human experience. As much as we'd like to try, we can't make people be in healthy relationship with us. More on this in the upcoming chapter on beginnings, middles and endings.

Conflict is experienced in lots of life's spaces, and despite what many of us believe, it cannot be avoided. I'm sure we'd prefer it to be different, but conflict can never be avoided, only stuffed down or ignored until it can't be. Years ago, my husband and I took our oldest child on their senior trip to Iceland. While we didn't drive around the entire island, the three of us made our way from Reykjavick to Vik and back in a rental car. At one particular point, we came around a bend and into a beautiful valley, alongside of which were mountains with what seemed like large holes in the sides of them. Out of the holes came huge plumes of steam. Iceland has been forming from volcanic eruptions for around 60 million years, so you can imagine what would happen if those mountains didn't have outlets for their steam. Most likely many more volcanic eruptions and Iceland would get a lot bigger.

Conflict is the same (also a great metaphor for self-regulation!). If we stuff conflict down, ignore it or armor up against it, there will eventually be uncomfortable eruptions. Eruptions can come in the form of behavior that creates disconnection, mental and physical illness and more, all because we aren't leaning into the benefits of managing conflict in healthier ways. Alternatively, we can tap our skills from the self-discovery chapters, like checking narratives with a thought triangle or using a Feel Good Plan to proactively and reactively calm our nervous systems. Add in a dash or two of the strategies you learn in the social awareness chapters, and you will be well on your way to taking your conflict navigation skills on the road and making conflict your bitch! A few reminders before moving on, as repetition helps form new wiring.

- Giving and receiving feedback (aka navigating conflict) is essential to healthy relationships.
- There's no magic to any of this, just good ol' fashioned skill-building through practice.
- No one "likes" conflict, but we usually hate it more when we don't have skills to navigate conflict or have have unhelpful stories around it .
- If you have emotional blocks to navigating conflict, create new thought triangles and practice them when (inevitably) conflict arises.
- Conflict comes in many forms and is usually accompanied by uncomfortable feelings. Tune into those feelings and soothe parts (usually our younger selves) feeling scared and unsure about what to say and how to resolve it.
- Differentiation in relationships, which can cause conflict at times, is healthy. Differentiation is the process of staying true to ourselves while staying in connection to our partners, etc. It means we develop and/or maintain autonomy while being in intimate relationship with others.
- If you fuck up, maybe you reverted to old, unhelpful ways of navigating conflict, it's okay! This is what repairs are for! You will learn more about repairs in the next chapter. Yes, I have an entire chapter dedicated to making repairs. You're welcome.

Let's set the stage for healthy conflict resolution. In the previous chapter, in the section on developing perspective-taking, I mentioned the concept of intent versus impact. This topic can bring up a lot of uncomfortable feelings and thoughts for some. This is one of the many times in this book I invite you to be open to possibility, and here's why. We are all humans just human-ing together. We are imperfect and make mistakes, and in order to learn and grow from those mistakes instead of making them over and over again, we need to acknowledge and be accountable for the negative impacts we have on others. I truly believe in general, a vast majority of humans have good intentions. I also believe in general, a vast majority of humans are good to their core. And we are imperfect and make relational and individual decisions not always in the best interest of ourselves or others. So in relationships, one of the most important aspects can be to focus on the impacts we have on each other.

If we all choose to make generous assumptions of ourselves and others, we will more likely be open to giving and receiving feedback, and taking accountability. Often, we push against feedback because shame stories tell us feedback means we aren't a good person. They tell us we are the opposite. My loves, this is not the case. Acceptance of our humanity will help us accept the humanity of others. Which means we can assume positive intent of ourselves and others AND still be accountable for negative impacts we have on ourselves and others.

Let's take this another layer deeper. How do you feel when someone impacts you negatively, and when you bring the impact to their attention, they answer with, "I didn't mean to," as if this absolves them from accountability? It can feel shitty right? If we assume positive intent of others, then it's assumed they didn't mean the impact, but they DID impact. They said or did the thing that wasn't okay, or they didn't say or do the relational thing. How can we be better humans if we are unwilling to be accountable when behavior doesn't align with values and has a negative impact on others? If we don't own our stuff, we can't shift our stuff. Bottom line, accountability is foundational to building or rebuilding trust, and trust is a huge part of providing safety within ourselves and our relationships. More on how to move forward with accountability in the next chapter.

Love Note: The way we experience feedback, because of the way our brains and bodies are wired, might lead us to gaslight, defend, offend or any other manner of defense mechanism. This is particularly relevant if you are a person who moves through the world with little to no pushback, most likely because you experience privilege of some kind. When we aren't practiced at receiving feedback, we are probably unskilled at handling it. We might experience feedback as an attack on our character, so we go on the offensive and attack. Could parts of you show up like this? If so, practice a new thought triangle. Begin with something like, "I'm working on new skills to manage discomfort when I get feedback I caused hurt or harm. I'm a good person and I can show this by being accountable. I can make mistakes and be okay." See how shifting our thoughts can shift the way we navigate receiving feedback? Remember, you're okay! You're a good human AND you're evolving. One of the most uncomfortable parts of this work is looking back at previous thoughts and behaviors and feeling the "ick" of them. Make repairs if needed, do the work to let go and stay present and future-focused. What is different and better because you're shifting what you think, say and do?

What if our stuff is wiring we aren't aware of? What if we don't know it's there until WE SAY OR DID THE THING? Should we still be accountable for what we said or did? Absolutely. Whether we consciously chose our wiring or not, it's our responsibility to examine and determine how to move forward. It may not be our fault the wiring is there (because of wiring other people and/or society installed), but it's our responsibility to shift wiring if it's harmful to ourselves and/or others. Shame is the root of our inability to acknowledge and repair harm, even for people with palpable egos like narcissists, who can move through the world causing harm right and left. Narcissism is a mask for insecurities arising from shame, and it can be tricky if you're navigating relationships with a narcissist, whether it's a characteristic, trait or an actual disorder. I'll put some resources in the Dive Deeper resources section to help with navigation of this challenge. We all have ego, though, so check yours around this issue by revisiting earlier chapters on Self-Discovery, or just by digging into a thought triangle about whatever is coming up for you.

Setting Up For Success

I offer an online parent support membership called SHIFT, and during one of our weekly community coaching calls, a SHIFT member brought a really valuable parenting dilemma to the group. They asked, "How do I give feedback to my teen with the least possibility of putting them on the defensive?" Does this dilemma sound familiar? If we don't have skills to navigate potentially difficult conversations, we might either come into conversations like this "hot," silence ourselves and/or walk on eggshells to avoid potential conflict. Here's the thing, giving and receiving feedback is ESSENTIAL to healthy relationships because it helps us be better parents, partners, friends, co-workers, and more. Without feedback we are just moving through relationships OUR way, which may not be THEIR way, and bottom line, might not be the best way. Navigating feedback also gives us opportunities to heal and grow parts of ourselves showing up in wonky (yet previously purposeful) ways. When the SHIFT community member brought their dilemma to the group, we discussed one strategy I consider to be the best when it comes to giving and receiving feedback. We also discussed additional things making this strategy even more successful. So, let's set you up for success as much as possible. I say as much as possible because we can't control the outcomes of conversations, we can only control what we think, say and do in interactions, so do your best AND let go of the rest. Try again. Have do-overs. Make repairs. You're human and so are the people you're connecting with.

So, when conflict arises in any form, consider these steps to set yourself up for success: pause and go inward, set the picnic, lead with curiosity, actively listen, have a clear agenda, bring notes to the picnic if necessary and collaborate on solutions if needed.

Breaking the Steps Down

Pause and go inward. Respond (or not), don't react then use your Feel Good Plan. I can't say this enough! A relational choice is to train your nervous systems to not overreact and make mountains out of mole hills. This may require using your Feel Good Plan, along with therapy, mentoring or coaching, really whatever it takes to heal those parts of you getting in the way of handling conflict, which again, is inevitable and even necessary and healthy in relationships. Ask yourself, "Is this really something I need to bring to a picnic or is it my own to tend to?" If it's your own to attend to, how will you do this? This step alone takes so much practice and is life work, but little by little, a little becomes a lot.

Approach your partner and **ask for a picnic.** Use your Feel Good Plan whether the person is ready or not to have a picnic. Don't have an expectation of the picnic happening right then. If anyone is dysregulated, or is getting close, put a pin in the conversation by saying something like, "Let's come back to this when we are ready. This is important and we both need to be in the headspace for it." Use your Feel Good Plan and return to the conversation as soon as possible.

Lead with curiosity. When the conversation happens, begin with and maintain CURIOSITY throughout. Use curiosity to gather more information, helping you have the possibility of dismantling stories and less-connecting patterns. This is the ONE STRATEGY I was talking about that will set you free in a lot of interactions. Questions like, "What do you think are the strengths in the report you wanted me to review?" or "How can I support you during this busy week so our family doesn't get derailed because of the stress level? Last week was really hard on all of us and I wonder if we can navigate it together better." Any of the questions from the Imago Dialogue section could be useful here, too. Be genuine and not condescending. Curiosity can also sound like starting conversations with, "Tell me more about ..." when you are thinking about an interaction and aren't quite sure what to make of it, even though your brain is trying hard to make meaning. Let your brain know you're going to gather more information, and until you do, it can chill with the storytelling (storytelling probably coming from a wounded place).

If you're on the giving or receiving end of feedback, take a breath, check your self-talk and use curiosity to your advantage. Curiosity and wonder are associated with the reward centers of our brains. The rewards center sends out all the feel good, yummy hormones and chemicals we want more of, like dopamine and serotonin, so really you're caring for your nervous systems by just getting curious. You can process more of the conversation afterwards if it's a particularly heavy topic for you.

Actively listen and pay attention to feelings that might be underneath and/or part of the feedback. Listen to what the person is really upset about. Don't grasp onto little details distracting from the issue. For example, "You're saying I wasn't thoughtful when I made plans last week without checking in with you first, but I made those plans two weeks ago not last week."

Have a **clear agenda and use "I" statements** such as, "I felt uncomfortable when you shared personal information about us at the party. We don't really know those people well enough yet and I'd like to wait to know them better before they know this about us" or "I think our morning routine (or lack of one) is really starting the day off wrong. Can we brainstorm some solutions and decide what can be done to make mornings feel more calm?" Practice the sentence stems and questions below in order to increase your chances of success.

I feel/felt …
I wonder if …
My concern is/was …
I would like to …
How/what do you feel/think about that idea?
Yes, I agree that … and at the same time …
I love you, and what you're saying and/or doing isn't okay. Can you try that again?

Bring notes to the picnic if necessary. Notes help us stay on track, be thoughtful with our words and stick to what is most important to discuss.

Collaborate on solutions if needed. Not every conflict requires a solution, but if you keep dancing around the same issue over and over again, you might consider building solutions. Connect with the person you're in relationship with and focus on solutions, not the problem itself. Which solution offers the most benefit and least amount of risk? Make solutions accessible, meaning they aren't "pie in the sky" and impossible to attain. An example of an inaccessible solution might be you would NEVER raise your voice again when you're in an argument with your kids or partner. An accessible solution would be you set up more reminders to use your Feel Good Plan throughout the day so your nervous systems don't get so maxed out you blow your top over every little thing.

Love Note: Lots of reminders and love notes about this because resolving conflict is a real sticking point in most relationships. Someone giving you feedback about something you said or did is not feedback about who you are as a person. A generous assumption we can all give each other is we are good humans. And the best humans sometimes say and do things that aren't okay. Notice what feelings come up and be with them, but don't get stuck in shame and blame. Shining a light on shame and blame by giving voice to them with safe people can help alleviate the weight of the feelings.

Now that you know how to prepare to navigate conflict, we need to dig into the tricky part (this does become less tricky) of making repairs. Before we do, here's another way to reframe feedback in order to help disrupt patterns of not seeing or hearing the person you're in relationship with. People who aren't invested in us don't bother giving feedback. They become passive aggressive, apathetic, use the slow fade or ghost you, because they either don't care enough about you to give feedback and/or they aren't skilled at giving it, so they don't.

Feedback means you matter to the other person. The person giving feedback WANTS to better the relationship, and giving and receiving feedback with whole hearts is one of the best ways to foster joy and connection. Eventually. Be patient and compassionate with yourself and others. Next time someone gives you relational feedback, tell yourself, "I matter enough for them to lean into the relationship and tell me this. I can listen and I can consider what they are saying and try to make things better. I can use my tools to handle how hard this is for me to hear."

Self-Reflection

- How did your caregivers navigate conflict? How about in your culture? What could you do differently and/or better?
- Identify some dark room shit you've navigated. How did you do it? How do you want to do it better in the future?
- Which step do you need to pay attention to the most when it comes to navigating conflict?
- Identify a lower-priority conversation you need to have. Walk through a dress rehearsal of the conversation in your mind, implementing the steps you read about in this chapter. Then practice by having the conversation!
- How do you think and feel about conflict now?
- What lyrics from *Don't Wanna Fight* by Alabama Shakes and *Blindsided* by Kelsea Ballerini do you think fit this chapter and why?

Affirmations

- I can show people they matter to me by practicing giving and receiving feedback in better ways.
- Managing conflict can lead to deeper, more joyful relationships. I'm up for it!

Dive Deeper Resources

CHAPTER 9

Make Conflict Your Bitch, Part Two

Listen to Something About You *by Level 42*

From where I stand, there's not much relationships can't recover from if BOTH PEOPLE choose to lean in. Friends, as sad as it may sound, the reality is sometimes we need to lean out of relationships because too much harm has been done and/or someone isn't interested in healing and growing alongside you. This is only for you to identify after deep self-reflection. But if both parties want to return to connection and rebuild trust, then making repairs is essential. As a society, though, we often suck at repairs. So, I'm going to simplify the practice to help you see immediate growth in your practice of making repairs. You probably have something at this moment you could make a repair for, right? I prefer to use the term repair as opposed to apology, because, as you'll see in this chapter, apologies are only one of the steps in making a repair. When we impact people negatively by causing hurt or harm, we create disconnection. The practice of making a repair helps us get back to connection. Depending on the level of hurt or harm, the repair process can take anywhere from a short conversation to months, or even years.

Before we dig into repairs, I want to acknowledge a few things getting in the way of genuine repairs. I'm making you aware of two things right off the bat so you can keep them in mind as you go through this chapter. Some people believe they don't need to apologize because, "This is just who I am," and it's the job of everyone else to accept them not apologizing or making changes. I call BULLSHIT. This type of mindset does not honor the human need to evolve and adapt. Adaptation means we make moves to level up our skill sets and be open to possibilities. There are probably areas in your life where you aren't leaning into healing and growing, and you're saying, "This is just the way I am" to avoid discomfort. Let's not do this anymore! Hello neuroplasticity! We are adults, and adults do uncomfortable things all the time. We got this.

Another reason genuine repairs don't happen is because our egos (connected to our wiring) tell us we have to be right. Why do you have to be right? What is underneath the need to be right? If you're not right, what does this trigger for you? Could it be the belief you're bad or there's something wrong with you? This is an opportunity for you to connect with your humanity and remember humans are good, to remember that sometimes humans say and do bad things. Doing something wrong doesn't mean there is something wrong with us. Our egos want to be right, but we should be careful we aren't operating from a place of ego because it's generally not a very relational way to be. If being right is a thing for you, pause and rework your thought triangle to something like, "I can make mistakes and be okay. I'm still a good human" (new thought) and notice you might feel more open and calm, causing you to show up (say and do = behavior) in more relational ways.

What if repairs don't matter as much to you as they do to the person you're in relationship with? Remember, we are learning to speak the love languages of the other person, and how they want to be in relationship, which means we make concessions if those concessions aren't at the expense of our well-being. If repairs matters to the other person and you care about them, this enough is reason to work through a repair.

Making Repairs

When we say or do disconnecting things, and want to get back to connection, the best way to do this is to learn the skill of making a genuine repair. Again, I prefer the term repair because I feel it is a more comprehensive term for what we want to accomplish. An apology can simply be a few words strung together and can be the quickest, lowest burden way to return to connection. Words, however, are most often not enough. We often need action behind our words in order to rebuild trust. Below are several non-examples and genuine examples of repairs.

Non-Example of a Repair: I have a deadline coming up for a huge work project, I'm caregiving for my ailing mom and it's tax season. I have a million things on my mind. Then, I raise my voice at my child in frustration because they didn't do a task I asked them to do.

Raising my voice doesn't align with my values, so I go to my child and say, "I'm sorry for raising my voice." They roll their eyes at me and say, "You keep saying sorry for the same thing. You always take your stress out on me." Essentially, my apology means little or nothing to them because of my behavior patterns. We end up not getting back to connection because my child doesn't trust I'm putting in the work to disrupt patterns.

Example of a Genuine Repair: I have a deadline coming up for a huge work project, I'm caregiving for my ailing mom and it's tax season. I have a million things on my mind. Then, I raise my voice at my child in frustration because they didn't do a task I asked them to do.

Raising my voice doesn't align with my values, so I go to my child and say, "I'm sorry for raising my voice. I notice when I'm stressed, I often take it out on you and it's not okay. I'm going to pay attention to this and work on managing my stress better. I think it's time to revisit my Feel Good Plan and up my game. Is there anything else I can do to make a repair?" He smiles, gives me a hug and we end up back in connection. Then I FOLLOW THROUGH on the actions I committed to.

Non-Example of a Repair: Tima comes home from work and notices her wife hasn't taken the trash out again even though it was her chosen responsibility. Tima walks in the door and immediately initiates a tense conversation with her wife about how she never does what she says she will do. Tima huffs off to their room leaving a swath of disconnection behind her. Notice, when we use extreme language in any context it can indicate younger parts of ourselves are showing up. Words like "always," "never," "no one," "everyone" and more are examples of extreme language, or black and white thinking.

Tima calms enough in her room to recognize she didn't practice her strategy of noticing the impact of the garbage not being out, pausing to take a note in her phone to save for their weekly check-in or if she feels it's more urgent, to set a picnic for a conversation about household responsibilities. She pops out, says, "I'm sorry for coming home like that but you keep not putting the trash out and then we have to deal with it piling up the whole week!"

Example of a Genuine Repair: Tima comes home from work and notices her wife hasn't taken the trash out again even though it was her chosen responsibility. Tima walks in the door and immediately initiates a tense conversation about how she never does what she says she will do. Tima huffs off to their room leaving a swath of disconnection behind her.

Tima calms enough in her room to recognize she didn't practice her strategy of noticing the impact of the garbage not being out, pausing to take a note in her phone to save for their weekly check-in or if she feels it's more urgent, to set a picnic for a conversation about household responsibilities. Tima remedies this by putting a note in her phone for their check-in time. She pops out, says, "I'm sorry for how I handled the interaction. What can I say or do to make a repair?"

Honestly, I could go on and on with non-examples and genuine examples of repairs, but I think you get the idea. So how do we do better?

Steps for Genuine Repairs

Steps for a genuine repair include the following, each of which I'll go into more detail on below: repair from a place of self-regulation, be specific, ask what you can do to make a repair and accept potential non-closure.

Breaking the Steps Down

First, **repair from a place of self-regulation.** Use your Feel Good Plan and other tools, like thought triangles, to get back to connection. The act of making a repair might bring on uncomfortable feelings, like shame, and you are developing the tools to manage your feelings. You've got this!

Second, **be specific about what you're apologizing for.** This confirms to the other person you "get it," so they feel seen and heard. This is a chance to practice accountability, which is essential to genuine repairs. Without accountability, you can have what feel like half-assed apologies exhibiting a lack of self-awareness and unskilledness. We often want to bypass this step to avoid discomfort. Choose not to bypass!

Third, **ask what you can do** to make a repair. Are words enough for the person you're apologizing to, or do they need action. Action might be necessary if what you're repairing has happened so many times that whatever you're doing, or not doing, to change the behavior isn't working. If what you are making a repair for has to do with racist, sexist, misogynist, classist or ableist behavior, then it's your human responsibility to do work around these things as part of the repair. This will massively build our self- and social awareness and cause less hurt and harm over time. I've put plenty of resources in this book you can dig into for help removing obstacles to people feeling safe, empowered and well.

Next, **how about a do-over as part of the repair?** Do-overs are my favorite! Do-overs are essentially a role-playing exercise where you get to exhibit skills you've been practicing. In do-overs, we want to identify where interactions went off the rails and course correct. This is your sliding door moment (see Dive Deeper Resources if you don't know what I'm referring to here). You can try again, together, to experience a different outcome. Do-overs are about taking accountability for what is yours and giving your brain an opportunity to see a different way of interacting. They are a dress rehearsal for next time and really help disrupt unhelpful relational patterns. We should be giving our brains lots of opportunities to see different and better ways, and do-overs help exponentially. Do-overs can begin with, "Next time I am super stressed, instead of ... I will …" Focus on changes in the future versus hashing out the should haves from the interaction you're doing over. Our brains should like this focus better because we can't change the past, but we can shift the future with intentional effort.

Lastly, **accept potential non-closure.** Repairs aren't magical fixes allowing people to move on right away. Repairs are a part of getting back to connection, but they aren't the end all, be all. Depending on the intensity and frequency of the hurt or harm, you might need several, or more, repair conversations before both parties experience the repair as complete.

Things to Keep in Mind

When forming repairs, there are a number of things to keep in mind to level up and guide your repair practice.

- **Separate apologies from feedback conversations.** Using Tima's example above, repair conversations are not the time to also give feedback. Let the words and actions of a repair settle into the other person's nervous systems to help you feel connected. Save feedback for your picnics and check-ins!
- **DO NOT put BUTs in your repair.** "But"s land as an excuse for behavior and/or as putting blame on the other person. You have not seen me put a DO NOT in this book yet, so take notice! An example of a but is, "I'm sorry I yelled at you, but you didn't put your things away and I've asked you to a million times!" We can do better by not having this word in our repairs.
- **Don't over-apologize** in your repair, or in general. Make it mean something when you make a repair by making them when it matters, and not for every little thing you perceive might have ruffled feathers. This could be a sign of people

pleasing, placating or porous boundaries. Own what is yours, and trust others are sovereign over their own bodies and experiences. It's not your job to make everyone around you comfortable at your own expense!

- **Communicate hurt and/or harm.** Those we are in relationship with shouldn't have to read our minds or miraculously know what happened wasn't okay, although each of us absolutely can do proactive work to learn fundamental things not okay to say or do. Some of those fundamentals, for example, are using certain words or phrases, invading the personal space of others and commenting on or touching someone else's body including their hair and/or pregnant belly. In other words, we can become aware of what most people generally deem okay or not okay in order to shift behavior if needed. At the same time, we can practice speaking our truth in a variety of ways so harm doesn't fester in our relationships and come out sideways, resulting in more harm.

What if you've made a genuine repair and the other person isn't responsive? While this can be distressing, some self-reflection might be in order. Has this repair been a pattern? Are there other issues causing the other person to not want to accept the repair? Remember, both people foster the third, the relationship itself. Relationships are not one-person shows! Invite the heartache, shame or disappointment to come closer (see Chapter Four) and be with the feelings. Doing so is part of human-ing, and with practices of connecting with and tending to your emotions, then shifting future behavior, you will navigate this in the best possible way. Here is an example of putting all of this into practice.

Person 1: I felt hurt when you snapped at me after I asked you a question. I'd like you to make a repair.

Person 2: I'm sorry I hurt you when I wasn't careful with my words and tone. How can I make a repair?

Person 1: I appreciate the apology. You can make a repair by giving me a hug and letting me know what you think you might do differently next time.

Person 2: <HUG> I hear you. I didn't get great sleep last night and didn't get to take my usual breaks at work today. I let stress creep in and didn't handle it well. I'll head to bed early tonight and make sure I take better care of myself tomorrow so I don't emotionally bleed all over you and the family when I come home.

Person 1: Okay, thank you for listening.

Notice, no buts in the apology, no excuses, nothing! Making repairs is not just about what TO say, they are also about what NOT TO say. Making repairs also goes beyond saying, "I'm sorry." Words matter little when there is no action behind them. Trust erodes when we apologize over and over again for the same or similar behavior (or don't apologize at all), without any meaningful effort put into preventing further harm.

I'd like to share another scenario very personal and dear to me. Recently, a good friend told me she was coming into town with a group of women I didn't know. Leading up to the visit, we'd talked about things they might want to do and, because my friend and I had gone to these places before and had a good time, and because I was invited along, I offered to get dinner and cigar bar reservations for the group. On the night of the reservations, I showed up to the restaurant but the group didn't. My friend texted me later they wouldn't make it to dinner, but she and the group would meet me later at the cigar bar. When I met them later, everyone's energy felt off, but I couldn't quite place why. Afterwards, they invited me out dancing, but then left and didn't tell me where to go or when to meet. My friend didn't answer subsequent texts. I felt really hurt, and old stories of rejection and abandonment came up. On the way home, I had a good cry, leaned on my Feel Good Plan and thought about how I might navigate the next time I spoke with my friend.

A few days later, before I'd had a chance to reach out, my friend texted and genuinely apologized. She said she wanted to talk on the phone about everything that happened. She then left a voice message with a short explanation of what had transpired during the visit. What she shared made a lot of sense, and I could then place the energy I was picking up at the cigar bar. In the voice message (I have it saved!) told me our friendship mattered a lot to her, and she should have just told me what was going on because she knew I would understand (accountability and being specific). She finished her message by asked me to call her back. Notice how she kept pursuing connection in order to make sure she was repairing the hurt (putting action behind her words). When I was able, I called her back and we had a really lovely conversation. Our chat meant A LOT, as I had recently been on the receiving end of hurt by others who had elected not to make a repair.

Since the phone call, my trust in her has only increased because she showed me she has the skill, will and capacity to make a genuine repair. I don't expect anyone to be perfect, but I do want people in my life who make genuine repairs. Letting go of the hurt was easier as a result of the repair, and our friendship is deeper and better because of how she initiated reconnection and how we both navigated the experience.

Forgiveness

I'm not a huge fan of the word forgiveness in the traditional sense of the word. Yup, I said it. I think we have warped perspectives on forgiveness, causing it to sometimes feel forced or expected. Sometimes it seems like forgiveness is a way for a person who harmed you to put the responsibility back on you in order for the relationship to return to connection. Forgiveness can also be a way for someone to bypass the hard work of making a repair, by simply asking for forgiveness instead. Someone might say things like, "I said sorry!" "Just get over it" or "Move on already" because they are uncomfortable sitting with impacts of the harm they caused, and if you forgive them they can be less uncomfortable. Others might encourage you to forgive someone because they are uncomfortable with your discomfort.

Yeah, that's a no for me. The version of forgiveness that speaks to me given what I've studied, as well as what I've personally and professionally experienced, is it can be a way for the person who was harmed to process and let go. I also like to reframe forgiveness as the acceptance of the reality of whatever harm occurred. Sometimes being stuck, which forgiveness or letting go can release us from, is because we are pushing back on the reality of what happened. Forgiveness may not involve the other person at all! Whatever you want to call forgiveness (I believe you get to decide), it can be an inner journey you are in control of. I encourage you to think, say or do whatever you need to do to resolve harm and conflict without pressure from others, or your own parts. To not allow others, or the interaction, to take up so much energy and mental load. Forgiveness can be a way for us to gain power back, if needed. I believe when we feel stuck, we often need to forgive ourselves for what our emotions and our parts are telling us the thing is about. If you've been significantly harmed and need help navigating the harm, I highly recommend connecting with a professional to support and guide you.

Forgiveness also doesn't have to mean the relationship goes back to the way it was. I once had a family member say, after a significant breach of trust, "I wish you could just forgive so we can move on and find peace in the relationship." I replied with, "I've already forgiven you, but this doesn't mean our relationship goes back to the way it was. I haven't seen much indication the behavior won't happen again, so I'd rather set a healthy boundary around how much we interact until I see signs things will be different." You can imagine this didn't land super well, but I released their reaction too, because it's my job to protect my emotional and psychological well-being by setting healthy boundaries.

Whatever your thoughts, feelings and beliefs are around forgiveness, I invite you to interrogate them to make sure they are your own. What were you taught to believe about forgiveness? Is it possible to forgive someone completely? What choices around letting go and self-forgiveness align with your values and belief systems? What shifts can you make to get unstuck and move forward when and how YOU want to? Not how others want you to.

- What were you modeled and taught regarding apologies, repairs, intent versus impact and forgiveness?
- What did you notice coming up for you as you read through the steps for making genuine repairs?
- Where can you increase your self-awareness and relational practices when it comes to repairs?
- What lyrics from *Something About You* by Level 42 do you think fit this chapter and why? Message me on social media and I'll select my three favorite responses to win a signed copy of the book!

Affirmations

- I can own what is mine in order for my relationships to be better. I have a better idea of what is mine after leaning into self-discovery.
- Making repairs benefits everyone involved, including me. I can forgive myself and get back to connection by doing the hard, but necessary, steps of making repairs.

Dive Deeper Resources

CHAPTER 10

Beginnings, Middles and Endings

Listen to Starting Over *by Chris Stapleton,*
Show and Tell *by Al Wilson and* Lost in the Light *by Bahamas*

I want you to picture your favorite library or bookstore. Is it the Beast's library in Beauty and the Beast? Or Changing Hands in Phoenix? How about The Seattle Public Library or the teeny, tiny bookstore in Pike Place Market (right across from my favorite donut hole stand)? Maybe Gabrielle Blair's (@designmom) library in her home in France? Have one in mind? Sit with the library or bookstore in mind, and then imagine every relationship you've ever had and everything you've ever experienced as a book in that library or bookstore. Each book has chapters filled with beginnings, middles and endings. Some books are super long, like Alex Haley's Roots long. Some are thin, taking up a sliver of space on the shelf. Then there's every type of book in between. We each have our own hypothetical library or bookstore, and we bring them with us into new relationships and experiences where we add even more books to our shelves.

I've been partnered for 25+ years and over that time, have written many chapters with a variety of beginnings, middles and endings. My husband sometimes jokes he's been married to five different women over the past 25 years, and I don't disagree with him. His joke speaks to our evolution as individuals and the evolution of our relationship, and we fully celebrate both. If we were the same people now we were in our early 20s, well shit, our brains weren't even fully developed then! If we were still operating from our early 20s wiring, well that's a lot of outdated wiring. No thanks!

Some of our shared books and chapters would be about experiencing infertility, adopting an older kiddo from foster care who came with a big life story, religious deconstruction, both of us finishing graduate school while raising a family, major family mental and physical health crises, several physical moves (Utah to Maryland to Washington to Arizona and more to come!) and a marriage separation, to name a few. We've also written an infinite amount of wonderful moments raising four beautiful humans, a bunch of feather mamas (chickens) and two fur babies (cats), and leaned into life and work fulfilling to us. We've come back from some very dark edges, and on the other side of those phases, we've experienced more depth and connection than we knew existed. I wouldn't want to take a single book off my shelf because I do believe in the beautiful paradox of life. All of our books and chapters are part of our story. What about yours? What would your books be about and what are you still writing?

Let's dig into what beginnings, middles and endings can look and sound like, as well as a few tips for navigating each with the social and emotional skill sets we've been developing.

New Relationship Energy, Everyone's Favorite Stage

Ah, the feels of meeting someone new! Excitement, anxiety, curiosity and stress, you get the idea! Depending on our wiring, meeting new friends, partners or whomever can be a lovely or not so lovely experience, and there are a few tools and strategies I'd like to share that can make new relationships even better. This chapter focuses mainly on partnered relationships and friendships, but you can take what feels applicable to other relationship structures as well.

Identify non-negotiables. What are three to five things you will not negotiate with a new friend or partner on? What truly matters to you? For example, my non-negotiables are we both practice self-awareness, have the desire to consistently heal and grow together and are open to possibility. These three things fit partnered relationships and friendships, but you can have different ones for any type of relationship.

Over the years, I've helped many clients determine their non-negotiables for new relationships. This way, they can evaluate potential relationships early on and not keep expending energy in ways compromising their desires, their sense of self and even their well-being. These are major energy leaks! Your work in this book so far should support more clarity around non-negotiables and hopefully, with some thoughtfulness, you'll be able to determine what your non-negotiables are. Do not settle for less than you need or want, because that's all you think you deserve. One of my very wise coaches, Barbra Orban, believes the concept of deserving to be a social construct, and that we actually just get to choose to deserve something. Or not (but definitely do choose to deserve anything you want). I wholeheartedly agree! As adults, we can choose the life we want for ourselves, including the relationships we want.

Pay attention in the early stages of any relationship. Be observant, curious and aware, but not hyper vigilant or operating from other wounds. Hypervigilance means there are parts of you on high alert for danger and you may make mountains out of molehills. The right amount of awareness and curiosity should suffice in keeping you out of danger without risking the relationship itself. It's one thing to think, "Hmm, I don't appreciate how they treat the strangers they encounter, like the servers at the restaurant we just ate at" versus something like, "I'm unsafe in this relationship because they are unkind to everyone" about the same experience. If they are, in fact, unkind to EVERYONE, do walk in the opposite direction!

Paying attention means we notice what comes up for us when we are in proximity to, and thinking about, our new relationship. Then, we can practice sifting through what is our stuff from past relationships (previous chapters help with this) and what are actually things we need to pay attention to. We won't see all the things, and we sometimes might be very surprised at some of the things we don't see. Take it from someone who, in general, reads people well. I've been surprised by new relationships a lot over the last few years, and when the surprise happens, the best we can do is chalk it up to experience, use strategies and tools to heal any new wounds created, or old wounds reopened, and take any learning into future relationships.

Noticing also means we **practice curiosity.** A lot of it! Ask questions and really listen. Think about what you learned about yourself in the section on self-discovery and get to know the wiring of your new friend or romantic interest. What are their love languages? Values? Beliefs? What lights them up and what drives them nuts?

Be realistic. Everyone has their shit and every relationship has tricky spots, because I believe being in connection with people is meant to draw attention to what we need to heal and grow. Notice if high expectations of others and perfectionism around friends and partners is a form of self-protection. Low standards in relationships can indicate a need to grow self-worth. What matters the most, in my mind, is if the person you're starting a relationship with has put effort into healing and growing and are doing what they can to not let their stuff bleed all over the relationship. Have they been in therapy? Read helpful books? Spent time self-reflecting about experiences and what they might want to shift? Along with your own boundaries, be sure to hold the right amount of space for people on their own healing and growing journeys.

Practice patience without giving in to self-doubt and other unhelpful wiring. Getting to know someone can take time, and the time can be perfectly lovely. What isn't lovely is when we hem and haw, overthink and distrust ourselves to navigate relationships in healthy ways. What can look like patience can actually be self-doubt, so drop into your body and check in with your parts to see what is really going on.

Use conflict as a litmus test for the relationship. Really! How one navigates conflict is a marker of their skill, will and capacity to foster healthy relationships. We might be sailing along, sometimes for quite a while, investing all kinds of energy (time, money) into the relationship and then conflict arises and BAM! We are knocked off our feet, sometimes not in a good way, by what they say and do. Hopefully we are pleasantly surprised by the bam, and the relationship train keeps chugging along, but many times it's the opposite. Either way, you acquired information you can use to guide your actions going forward.

Show up as yourself from the very beginning instead of being who you think they want you to be. This does not mean you divulge all your deepest, darkest secrets right away, because practicing boundaries means realizing not everyone is safe with your story. But you can certainly be yourself, even if you're still discovering who you are, in initial encounters.

Remember, a healthy relationship is a THIRD, meaning you each bring your authentic selves to the space and then develop the relationship (the third) together. This means eventually you need to be present in all your full, authentic glory, with all your shit (that you're, ahem, intentionally healing and growing) in addition to all your strength and gorgeousness. Yes, different people bring out different parts of us, which is perfectly normal and healthy, but showing up as someone you're not is unsustainable, exhausting and a waste of everyone's time, especially yours. Find people who you can truly be yourself with. Test the waters early on. Be honest in your Hinge or Bumble BFF profiles in order to sift through the people who aren't for you. When I moved to Phoenix a few years ago, I got on Bumble BFF, shared my values and what types of friends I was looking for in my profile and ended up meeting some of the best humans I know. It can be so liberating to just BE YOURSELF.

Love Note: Dr. Maya Angelou said, "When people show you who they are, believe them." I absolutely agree AND there are people who are so good at masking who they really are that sometimes we can have very unpleasant (to put it lightly) experiences when we find out who someone really is. This usually happens after harm has been done, and we see if they navigate it with grace and compassion or not. Be kind to yourself when this happens. Tune inward, and tend to your emotions and well-being. This is part of our humanity. We can be messy, miss the mark AND still be okay. In fact, we can actually live an incredibly rich life while still being beautiful messes. The last thing we need to do is sharpen those hard edges with self-flagellation. Instead, let's soften our edges with self-compassion, and THAT my friends, is what will help us move through tough relational experiences.

If you didn't adhere to these suggestions for a healthy beginning of a relationship and find yourself in a relationship pickle, it's not too late to make a shift. You have options! Neither me or my partner took those suggestions into account because we were 23 and 20 when we married. No joke! We've done a lot of pivoting throughout our relationship and that relational move invites a lot of options. Another possibility includes riding it out for a bit longer until you collect more data as you practice the suggestions above. Ending the relationship and starting over with another friendship, partnership, etc. Just know that you always, always have choices. Sometimes it can just take a bit to see what those choices are.

Middles, aka Relationship Chapters

Middles really need some extra love. The new relationship energy has worn off and life can be rather mundane. Routine. Lifeless. We aren't saying the things we need to say and are setting patterns of under-communication, which can lead to misunderstandings and uncomfortable feelings. Maybe we notice we're losing important pieces of ourselves as we move further into the relationship. When we are in these ruts, we need to shake things up in order to not lose ourselves and our relationships in work, kids or anything else sucking the life out of us. If you haven't already, this is a great time to implement scheduled check-ins, which is one structure to have in place as you develop healthier communication and navigate more difficult conversations, or any conversation really. Think about being really intentional in the middles, because the middles are where it can be easy to move through life on autopilot. We need focused attention to disrupt thought and behavior patterns that are meh, but could be better!

Middles are also a great time to think outside the relationship box in ways aligning with your beliefs and values. One of the ways to spice up the middles is by restructuring your partnership or friendship. Relationships can be a creative process, and there are many structures in which partnered relationships, in particular, can thrive. From traditional monogamous structures with two people in the same household, to monogamous couples who have sleep divorces (google it!), to open and polyamorous relationships, to the many other options and probably some options I'm not even aware of! Whatever two (or more) consenting adults choose is right and true for them, is right and true. The world is your oyster, and with some creativity and imagination, you and your partner can decide what works for you both. Restructuring a relationship could be exactly what you need to write a new chapter in your lives!

Maybe restructuring isn't necessary, but you and your friend, partner or kid need a boost or a reset? Has it been a while since you had FUN? Something pushing at the edges of your comfort zone? Something middles often lack is novelty. We fall into routines to help our nervous systems feel safe, but those routines might not provide enough of the feel good chemicals we want. There are endless ways to intentionally infuse our everyday lives with more excitement. Notice how your mood and ability to connect improves as you try new things! This suggestion might seem silly or cliche, but believe me it's not. As adults, we often pay way too much attention to the things we have to do versus the things we want to do, such as doing something fun or learning something new. Let's make adulting look more attractive to kids, shall we? Otherwise, it's no wonder they grow up and don't want to launch into adulthood.

Look online to find ideas on how to shake things up and add novelty to your life and relationships. Even little things, like trying a new food, changing up your order at the coffee shop, taking a new route to work, reading a new book genre or walking a new trail can go a long way in spicing up your relationships. You can add novelty with others, but you can also do some things on your own. Solo adventures can add a little (or a lot) spice to relationships because you'll have new things to share! If you feel like you've already lost yourself a bit, make some shifts to find yourself again.

This is a great time to practice the art of differentiation I mentioned in the chapter on conflict. We can have beautiful partnerships with people who move through life in different ways as long as we are mutually respectful, everyone is consenting and the ways we move through life aren't causing harm. Do you and your relationship partner have different spiritual beliefs, politics, hobbies and/or social batteries? With some skill, will and capacity, these dissimilarities don't have to be deal breakers. Remember those five women my husband says he's been married to? He says this because I've had many of my own chapters with beginnings, middles and endings, largely in part to our ability to differentiate. It's a really wonderful part of being human when we can keep discovering different parts of ourselves and each other. We can find out what makes us tick as we enter new chapters, end old ones and dig into those middles. They can be so juicy!

Endings

I hope you've noticed how intentional I've been in this book, and in this chapter in particular, about focusing on healthy relationships versus long relationships. We all know people who've been friends or partners for forever, but their relationships are far from healthy. Longevity is not the hallmark of a good relationship. Length can be an important component of some relationships, but it isn't essential to experiencing all the joy and connection coming from a relationship. Remember, we can have thin books or long books on our bookshelves, and everything in between! Some of your books might be a quicker read than others, but none are better or worse than any other. They just ARE.

There are sometimes relationships, or certain points in a relationship, where you will have few reasons to stay and a million reasons to leave, or vice versa. At the same time, if all parties involved are willing to keep pushing by tapping into resources like therapy, coaching and self-development (especially if you're a parent), then an ending could be delayed in the short-term and maybe even over the long-term. If there are children involved in a relationship contemplating an ending, I sincerely hope the adults caring for those kids do everything within their power to model and teach healthy relationship patterns to such vulnerable humans. Healthy modeling can happen whether those involved stay together and write new chapters OR end the book. Staying together for the sake of children should not be enough of a reason to be together. If you stay together, but continue to model and teach thought and behavior patterns children will need to undo later on, I question the value of staying together. Sometimes healthy and whole (at least working on it) individuals who have separated are better models to children than people who stay together and continue to do harm.

If you are facing a potential ending to a relationship, consider the following strategies and tools to help you navigate the waters: develop a cost-benefit analysis for your relationship, spend a lot of time in self-reflection and with trusted support, choose your village wisely, try different decisions on for size, let go of what you need to in order to heal and grow and zoom out to get a helpful perspective.

Breaking It Down

Develop a cost-benefit analysis for your relationship. Essentially you want to dig into what fills your bucket and what doesn't. Write what comes to mind in different columns so you can see it clearly on paper. Be very honest with yourself. If you're not brutally honest, you're only abandoning yourself in the long-run, and no one is worth abandoning yourself for. You might, for example, be doing mental gymnastics to make a particular relationship, job or even religion work, and seeing columns on paper can provide the clarity you need. Do this exercise with a trusted friend (obviously not the person you might be ending things with) or your therapist if you're having a hard time with it. Don't forget to factor in the costs and benefits connecting to your mental, emotional, spiritual and physical well-being.

Spend a lot of time in self-reflection and with trusted support. There can be a million reasons to consider an ending to a relationship, or there could be just one. With people we care deeply about, we don't want to take such important decisions lightly. Dig deep and ask yourself helpful questions like, "What part of this is mine? What parts are not mine and I can hand back to the other person? How did I facilitate how we got to this point? If I stay, what will need to be different I can invite myself and the other person to lean into? If I go, what do I imagine will be different and/or better?" Remember, everywhere you go, there you are, so if you haven't intentionally tried to heal and grow, your thought and behavior patterns, and wounds from past relationships, will follow you. Time spent in self-reflection and with an attitude of curiosity can be very soothing to our nervous systems, so muster up as much curiosity as possible to nurture them so you can make decisions from a regulated place. A lack of personal safety being the exception.

Choose your advisors wisely. This may not be the time you want auntie's or sister's or your hair dresser's advice on what to do in the relationship, so be careful who you disclose relationship issues to. You need a special kind of village (always!) for significant relationship issues, so make sure you choose people who are not flame fanners and who are willing and capable of helping you face the music if needed. There are very few people, outside of the person I'm having the issue with, who I talk to about relational issues and one of them is my therapist! Because therapists need therapists too.

Try different decisions on for size. I want you to visualize choices as different outfits you get to try on. Picture yourself in a dressing room, with lots of options hanging on the hooks. You try on each item, and some of them you take right off because of how it feels or looks on your body. The tag is scratching you, the waist is too tight, the butt is too saggy or the hem is a bit too long. Other items you put on and check yourself in the mirror longer because they just look and feel SO GOOD. Then there are items you hang on the maybe hook, because you aren't yet sure how you feel about them, or where you'd even wear them. The same is true for decisions! When we try on decisions, our bodies will give us information to help guide us towards the best decision. You'll have your hell no, your hell yes and your maybe decisions, all of them offering information helping you move forward.

This is an exercise I run clients through regularly. Let's say you've done all the self-reflection possible, and now you've come to some potential conclusions. You've got some options on the table, even if some of the options feel like shitty ones. Then, you get in your head with your stories and try to make decisions from a place not including your body in the decision-making. You get stuck, because talking yourself in and out of decisions can be easy to do. We can't only think our way through these kinds of decisions, we also have to feel our way through, so this is a more embodied practice allowing our bodies, holding so much wisdom, to help us make big life decisions. Here's how it might look.

- Sit comfortably in a chair, take some deep breaths and connect to your body in ways feeling comfortable to you. Next, see how each of the options you are weighing, one at a time, FEELS to your body. For example, if you say out loud or to yourself, "I'm staying in this relationship/job/religion," what do you notice happens in your body? What do your parts say? What sensations are you having? This is just data collection, so focus on just gathering information.

- Next, tell yourself (for example), "I'm leaving. It's time to go" and sit with the decision for a few moments. How does the decision feel? If there are more options for whatever decision you're facing, keep trying them on one at a time until you've cycled through all of them. What did your body tell you is the best choice for you? Tuning into your body, and coupling this with a lot of thought, is hands down the best way to make decisions in my opinion. It's not always super clear at first, and you might need to do this several times, but good decisions can often be made using this process.

Let go of what you need to in order to heal and grow. We don't want to hang onto things no longer serving our well-being. This can be thoughts, feelings, behaviors, relationships, jobs, belief systems, too tight pants, anything really. If we hang on too long, energy leaks in our life could become overwhelming, and this is decidedly not a great way to live. When we let go of what no longer serves us, we experience more room for what we want more of, like joy, love, self-love, capacity, faith, authenticity, healing and growing. In other words, all the good stuff!

An important belief to let go of is we must be liked by everyone in order to be okay. I am very sure I'm not everyone's cup of tea, as I've gotten this feedback indirectly and directly! Now, I might know this in my head, but there are still parts of me wanting everyone to like me. But I, myself, don't personally gel with everyone, so why should I expect everyone to gel with me? It's okay, you're still lovable and likable! You're still good enough. Don't try to force something that isn't meant to be.

Zoom out on your life to gain helpful perspective. When we are in the thick of navigating life's trickier moments, we might have a hard time seeing what is possible. Spend some time in mindful visualization, zooming out of the situation you're in so you can see the big picture. When we toggle back and forth in our mind's eye between what is and what can be, we are more likely to see a path forward.

Unskilled Endings

There are lots of ways to handle a relationship ending, and some of them are just plain not okay. Here are a few we want to avoid.

Ghosting. I hear examples of this all the time in my therapy practice, and I've experienced it too. Just say the thing, whatever it is, before you stop communicating. Ghosting is what teens do to each other, so as adults let's move beyond this unskilled strategy. Examples of things you might say instead of ghosting are, "I'm just not feeling a connection but I wish you the best," "I've got a lot going on right now, I'll reach back out when I have capacity," or "I'm upset with something you said when I saw you last." There are so many better options than dropping another human like a hot potato.

Not even trying to manage the conflict. Navigating conflict, and just saying the thing, requires skill, will and capacity on everyone's part. We need to know how to do this, we need to want to do this and we need to have bandwidth in our nervous systems and schedules to do this. Unfortunately, sometimes skill, will and capacity don't match up and these conversations never happen. You're developing your skill, will and capacity, so I imagine this isn't you? If it is, do you need to make a repair while still maintaining your boundary?

Leaving in a blaze of glory. Some people just can't navigate an ending without burning the house down first. They blast the other person on social, tell too many people about the shitty thing the other person did, try to have the last word by name-calling or being cruel and/or try to take things that aren't theirs for their own benefit. If it's truly a sound decision to end a relationship, take the skilled path of only leaving with what is yours. This can sometimes get muddy in a divorce or separation, and might need to be navigated with legal representation, but otherwise, do your best to leave a relationship with grace and compassion for all involved.

Love Note 1: Darlings, an all-too-common, unfortunate ending or potential ending to a relationship is a parent unwilling to do the work to develop and maintain relationships with their adult child(ren). Estranged or strained relationships with a parent, as an adult, can be a painful experience, so we want to practice all the tools and strategies we've discussed so far to navigate these situations. Be soft with yourself. Tend to your emotions and your parts. Practice showing up in ways aligning with your values and I et go of the rest. Set boundaries to protect and foster your well-being. We can't make people do the work to be able to show up for us in healthy ways. We can only be sovereign over our own experience. If you'd like to get more support, one of my favorite books around this dynamic is Adult Children of Emotionally Immature Parents, which can be found in the Dive Deeper resources at the end of this chapter.

Love Note 2: My friends, if you are in any relationship with a narcissist, especially people who have Narcissistic Personality Disorder or similar, you will need lots of love and support to navigate middles and/or complete an ending. There are lots of books and other resources available and I highly suggest digging into them, because ending something with a narcissist is a whole different ball game, especially if you're co-parenting. Practice lots of self-compassion, and protect yourself with knowledge on how to manage these types of endings in ways protecting your psychological, emotional and physical safety. Get a really good lawyer who knows how to deal with these types, then take yourself to therapy. There can be a lot of wounds to heal from.

Nature offers us example after example of how life is about seasons, growing, evolving, beginnings, middles and endings, and so much more. As human beings, we are not exempt from having these experiences! When we are open to the rhythm of life's chapters, often most acutely felt in relationships, and build the necessary skills and resources, we can manage everything with much more grace and compassion.

Love Note 3 (because this chapter deserves lots of love notes): For every ending there is a beginning. Read this again and again. Endings feel so scary because what we leave behind is KNOWN, to both our brains and bodies. My loves, possibility also lies in the UNKNOWN, and maybe (definitely) there could be more joy and deeper connections waiting to enter your life. Ask yourself questions like the following when a beginning or ending presents itself: What can I create with this beginning or ending? What could be different or better? What haven't I experienced yet but want to try? How will I meet the needs the person I'm ending something with previously met? How can I practice self-trust and love myself even more through this? Ending something not in your highest good is a sign of self-trust and should be honored. This does not mean it won't be agonizing, heartbreaking or devastating, as well as all of the other most uncomfortable feels. Remind yourself to also pay attention to the possibilities, though. Beginnings can be magical.

Self-Reflection

- What were you modeled and taught about what partnered relationships should look and sound like? What about work relationships? Parent/child relationships?
- What were you modeled and taught about middles, endings or any type of shift in relationships?
- Identify some beautiful beginnings after some tough endings. Find even the tiniest of things to anchor to.
- What lyrics from *Starting Over* by Chris Stapleton, *Show and Tell* by Al Wilson and *Lost in the Light* by Bahamas do you think fit this chapter and why?

Affirmations

- Every ending also means a beginning. I can't wait to see what new beginnings hold for me. I'm grateful for the choice I have to lean into them.
- I can let go of what isn't filling my bucket to make more room for what is, and can refill my bucket.
- I'm creating safer, more joyful spaces for myself and others. I have a lot to offer anyone!

Dive Deeper Resources

CHAPTER 11

My Final Love Note

Listen to Turn Your Love Around *by George Benson*

*Final Love Note: My darling readers, thank you for coming on this journey with me! My wish for you is you begin, little by little, to capture more and more joy and connection through your own healing and growing. I wish for you more self-trust, with which you can experience more calm, confidence and capacity to truly LIVE, not just exist. In doing so, I wish for you to be part of healing and growing as a global community by creating healthier relationships. I don't think there is an individual or world problem we couldn't solve if every human practiced more self-awareness, self-management and social awareness, so I'm grateful you're in this space to start or do more of just this. Life is beautiful and wildly tricky at the same time, and yet, even when navigating the roughest of waters, with a little more skill, will and capacity, **it can be better!***

Self-Reflection

- What did you think and feel about yourself before reading this book? How about after reading the book?
- What did you think and feel about your life so far before reading this book? How about after reading the book?
- What did you think and feel about relationships before reading this book? How about after reading the book?
- How do you want your relationships to FEEL more often?
- What do you need to shift (little by little) in what you think, say and do to guide your relationships in the direction you want? Remember it takes two (or more) to tango AND we can shift our relationships a lot just by doing our own work.
- What lyrics from *Turn Your Love Around* by George Benson do you think fit this chapter and why? Message me on social media and I'll select my three favorite responses to win a signed copy of the book!

Affirmations

- Compile all of the affirmations you chose into one space and practice, practice, practice them until they feel more and more true for you!

Dive Deeper Resources

How to Help

I truly believe the concepts in this book can help anyone and everyone make their lives and relationships better, and I hope you feel the same! Here are some ways you can help me get the word out.

- Feature my book at your next book club
- Contact local bookstores and libraries and ask them to carry my book on their shelves and websites
- Contact local bookstores and libraries and ask them to host a book signing/reading event
- Share my book, and/or your experience with my book, on social media
- Tell all the people in your life about my book!
- Gift my book to high school and college graduates, your family and friends, your colleagues and bosses
- Join my **online book club** where we, as a community, dig deeper into the material and other resources
- Host an event such as a book signing/reading, I'd love to travel around and meet you!
- Hire me to speak at an event for your company or organization

Finally, I'd love to hear from you! Email your answers to self-reflection questions, or anything else you'd like to share, to me at <u>cher@cheranderton.com</u>. I'll see you in book club!

Works Referenced

2Pac, Debarge, B., Steward, D.B., Arnaud, D. (1995). I Ain't Mad At Cha [Recorded by 2Pac and Danny Boy]. On 2Pac Greatest Hits. Death Row Records. (1996)

ACEs Too High (n.d.) What ACEs Do You Have? Retrieved on March 27, 2022 from https://acestoohigh.com/got-your-ace-score/

Alabama Shakes, Howard, B. (2016). Don't Wanna Fight [Recorded by Alabama Shakes]. On Sound & Color. ATO Records. (2016)

Asian Pacific Institute on Gender-based Violence (n.d.). Patriarchy & Power. Retrieved on April 15, 2022 from https://www.api-gbv.org/about-gbv/our-analysis/patriarchy-power/

Beck, A., Beck, J. (2020). Cognitive Behavioral Therapy: Basics and Beyond (3rd ed.). The Guilford Press.

Burke Harris, N. (2018). The Deepest Well: Healing the Long-Term Effects of Childhood Adversity (1st ed.). Mariner Books.

Butler, A., Chapman, J., Forman, E., Beck, A. The empirical status of cognitive-behavioral therapy: A review of meta-analyses. Retrieved from: https://www.sciencedirect.com/science/article/abs/pii/S027 2735805001005

Carlisle, B., Hemby, N., McKenna, L. (2019). Crowded Table [Recorded by The Highwomen]. Elektra Records. (2019)

Carroll, L. , (2020). 6 Problems With The Love Languages, From A Couples Therapist. Retrieved from https://www.mindbodygreen.com/articles/ways-youre-thinking-about-the-love-languages-wrong

Center for Disease Control (2023). Adverse Childhood Experiences. Retrieved from https://www.cdc.gov/violenceprevention/aces/index.html

Champlin, G., Graydon, J., Lukather, S. (1981). Turn Your Love Around [Recorded by George Benson]. On the George Benson Collection. Warner Bros.

Cherry, K. (2022). What is Neuroplasticity? Retrieved from https://www.verywellmind.com/what-is-brain-plasticity-2794886

Cleveland Clinic: The Parasympathetic Nervous System: Retrieved from: https://my.clevelandclinic.org/health/body/23266-parasympathetic-nervous-system-psns

Cohn, R. (2021). Working with the Developmental Trauma of Childhood Neglect: Using Psychotherapy and Attachment Theory Techniques in Clinical Practice (1st ed.). Routledge.

Collaborative for Academic, Social, and Emotional Learning (CASEL). (n.d.) What is the CASEL Framework? Retrieved March 23, 2022, from https://casel.org/fundamentals-of-sel/what-is-the-casel-framework/#social-awareness

Cowings, E.; Baker Most, J.; Cowings, E.M.B. (2015). Distance [Recorded by E. King]. On The Switch. Making Music Records. (2014)

Cube, Ice (1992). Check Yo Self [Recorded by I. Cube and DAS EFX]. On The Predator. Priority Records. (1993)

Dana, D. (2020). Polyvagal Exercises for Safety and Connection: 50 Client-Centered Practices (1st ed.). W. W. Norton & Company.

Eilish, B. O'Connell, F. (2020). My Future [Recorded by B. Eilish and F. O'Connell]. On Happier Than Ever. Santa Monica, CA: Darkroom/Interscope Records. (2020)

Hasa. (n.d.) What is the Difference Between Competencies and Skills? Retrieved on March 23, 2022 from https://pediaa.com/what-is-the-difference-between-competencies-and-skills/

Hendrix, H., Lakelly Hunt, H. (2019) Getting the Love You Want: A Guide For Couples (Updated ed.). St. Martin's Griffin.

Joseph, F. (2022). Patriarchy Blues: Reflections on Manhood (1st ed.). Harper Perennial.

Kearney, B., Price, R. (2018). I Can Change [Recorded by Lake Street Dive]. On Free Yourself Up. Nonesuch.

King, M., Lindup, M., Gould, P., Gould, R., Badarou, W. (1985). Something About You [Recorded by Level 42]. On World Machine. Polydor Records.

Lenroot, R. and Giedd, J. (2022). The Changing Impact of Genes and Environment on Brain Development During Childhood and Adolescence: Initial findings from a neuroimaging study of pediatric twins. Retrieved from https://pubmed.ncbi.nlm.nih.gov/?

term=LENROOT%20RK%5BAuthor%5D

Levine, A., Heller, R. (2012). Attached: The New Science of Adult Attachment and How It Can Help You Find and Keep Love (Reprint ed.). TarcherPerigee.

Lieberman, M. (2013). Social: Why Our Brains Are Wired To Connect (1st ed.). Crown.

Mate´, G. (2022). The Myth of Normal: Trauma, Illness & Healing in a Toxic Culture (1st ed.). Vermilion.

Mate´, G. (2011). When the Body Says No: The Cost of Hidden Stress (1st e.). Wiley.

McGonical, K. (2015). The Upside of Stress: Why stress is good for you and how to get good at it (2nd ed.) Avery.

Menakem, R. (2017). My Grandmother's Hands: Racialized Trauma and the Pathway to Mending Our Hearts and Bodies. Central Recovery Press.

Metzl, J. (2019). Dying of Whiteness: How the Politics of Racial Resentment is Killing America's Heartland (1st ed.). Basic Books; American.

Oluo, I. (2020). Mediocre: The Dangerous Legacy of White Male America. Seal Press.

Petty, J. and DSTL. (2023). I Like Me [Recorded by Propaganda]. On Terraform: The Possibility. San Francisco, CA: EMPIRE Records.

Reese, K. (2019). Nurture Versus Nature: The Timeless Debate. Retrieved from https://www.researchgate.net/publication/331155182_Nature_ Versus_Nurture_The_Timeless_Debate

Ross, H. (2018). Our Search for Belonging: How our need to connect is tearing us apart (Illustrated ed.). Berrett-Koehler Publishers.

Roysamb, E. and Bang Nes, R. (2018). The Genetics of Well-being. Retrieved from https://www.researchgate.net/publication/322636816_The_ge netics_of_wellbeing

Santos-Longhurst, A. (n.d.). There Are 5 Love Languages — Here's How to Find Yours. Retrieved from https://www.healthline.com/health/love-languages

Schwartz, Heather L., Michelle Bongard, Erin D. Bogan, Alaina E. Boyle, Duncan C. Meyers, and Robert J. Jagers. Social and Emotional Learning In Schools Nationally and in the Collaborating Districts Initiative: Selected Findings from the American Teacher Panel and American School Leader Panel Surveys. Retrieved from https://www.rand.org/pubs/research_reports/RRA1822-1.html.

Schwartz, R. (2021). No Bad Parts: Healing Trauma and Restoring Wholeness with the Internal Family Systems Model (1st ed.). Sounds True.

Sebastian, J., (1965). Do You Believe In Magic [Recorded by the Lovin' Spoonful]. Kama Sutra.

Statista (n.d.). Number of Mass Shootings in the United States Between 1982 and April 2023, By Shooter's Gender. Retrieved on January 3, 2023 from https://www.statista.com/statistics/476445/mass-shootings-in-the-us-by-shooter-s-gender/

Suzuki, W. and Fitzpatrick, B. (2016). Healthy Brain, Happy Life: A Personal Program to Activate Your Brain and Do Everything Better (Reprinted Edition). Dey Street Books.

The Window of Tolerance: Supporting the well-being of children and young people. Retrieved from: https://www.gov.je/SiteCollectionDocuments/Education/ID%20The%20Window%20of%20Tolerance%2020%2006%2016.pdf

Vanderheym, A., Ballerini, K. (2023). Blindsided [Recorded by K. Ballerini]. On Rolling Up the Welcome Mat. Black River.

Vandross, L. (1981). Never Too Much [Recorded by L. Vandross]. On Never Too Much. Santa Monica, CA: Epic Records. (1981)

Warren, D.E. (1989). If I Could Turn Back Time [Recorded by Cher]. On Heart of Stone. Los Angeles, CA: Geffen Records.

Yanez, A., Schaeman, D., Easton, E., Meshorer, O., (2021). This is how i learn to say no [Recorded by EMELINE]. On What It Means to Be a Girl. Sony/ATV Music.

Author Bio

Cher Anderton (she/her) is a Licensed Clinical Social Worker in Washington and Arizona. Cher is a passionate speaker, parent coach and therapist who, in addition to this work, offers employee wellness support and parent education to companies, organizations and individuals through consulting and an online parent education membership. Cher has helped countless humans grow their social and emotional fluency so they can experience more joy and connection in their personal and professional lives! Outside of work, Cher can be found missing her children who have flown/are flying the coop, digging into community work, flying to see other people she misses, dreaming up DIY projects and adventuring anywhere and doing anything that doesn't involve heights. Great food, great company and great conversation are three of her most favorite things, especially when they all come together!

You can find out more about Cher and stay in touch with her through her newsletter at cheranderton.com.

www.ingramcontent.com/pod-product-compliance
Lightning Source LLC
Chambersburg PA
CBHW071312140726
47996CB00005B/1733